Caroline S. Whitmarsh

Hymns of the Ages

First Series

Caroline S. Whitmarsh
Hymns of the Ages
First Series
ISBN/EAN: 9783337405014

Printed in Europe, USA, Canada, Australia, Japan

Cover: Foto ©Thomas Meinert / pixelio.de

More available books at **www.hansebooks.com**

HYMNS OF THE AGES.

BEING

SELECTIONS FROM LYRA CATHOLICA, GERMANICA
APOSTOLICA, AND OTHER SOURCES.

WITH AN INTRODUCTION
By REV. F. D. HUNTINGTON, D. D.

FIRST SERIES.

BOSTON:
TICKNOR AND FIELDS.
M DCCC LXI.

PREFACE.

IT has been our purpose in compiling this volume, to bring together, irrespective of creed and in a convenient form, some of the best sacred poetry, such as contains quiet thoughts for quiet hours,—devotional, comforting, peaceful.

We have therefore in several instances omitted hymns which deservedly rank among the best, and in those from the Lyra Catholica have made a few slight alterations.

Preferring the older hymns as less known, and richer in association, we have not limited ourselves to these: whatever seemed to belong in the book we have placed here, not carelessly, yet caring little for its outward source. If it be true that all along the ages and amid all varying phases of belief, the human heart is the same, and if THIS in the hymns before us, has chanted its yearnings, and doubts, and comforts, and heavenward hopes, in the one great temple whose roof overarches all our creeds, need we ask whether the strain first stole from desk or aisle, from monkish crypt or kingly chapel, from the soul of a heart-broken sinner, or canonized saint?

The heart of humanity in its highest, deepest moods has spoken here, still speaks; and the Divine heart has listened, listens still as we believe, to these tender and glorious songs.

C. S. W
A. E. G.

JULY, 1858.

PREFACE

TO THE LYRA CATHOLICA.

COMPETENT and willing hands have been found to do the grateful work of making these selections of rare and beautiful poetry. Most of the pieces, not all, are culled from the rich and hallowed minstrelsy of the Catholic Communion,— the time being quite come when Christians who would be truly catholic, cannot afford to lose the nourishment and consolation for the inward life, which any branch of Christ's Body supplies. To most Protestants these pieces will be new. By a few, some of them will be greeted as acquaintances already familiar and endeared, the companions of many sacred hours. The present writer's office is merely to pass on to the public what the taste and veneration of two friends have made ready. Without undertaking to commend these noble and graceful productions, he would only invite the inquiry whether the elements and influences united in them, are not precisely such as the religious culture of our time and region needs; whether the nameless quality of genuine sacred poetry is not in them, in a remarkable measure; whether the energy and fire of original genius are not finely blended with the simplicity of a quiet heart and a deep spirituality; whether the facts, the materials, the symbols, the persons, all the outward forms and events through which the Eternal Word is revealed, are not here so delicately and vigorously touched as to render them powerful attractions to a holy life; and whether devotion is not likely to grow ardent and firm where the inmost soul of man is so humbly thrown open, as here, to the personal approaches of his Maker and Redeemer.

It may be interesting to those readers who are first introduced to the treasures of devout poetry in the Old Church by this volume, to know that the *Lyra Catholica* most in use in this country is a republication and enlargement of an English collection, of the same name, compiled and translated by Edward Caswall in 1849,—extracts from whose preface are given below. The American work is published by Edward Dunigan and brother, of New York, whose kindness and courtesy in allowing the present abridgment are cordially acknowledged. It includes three parts : 1. The Hymns of the Roman Breviary and Missal, with others adapted to the annual Festivals of the Church; 2. Hymns, Anthems, and Holy Lyrics, appropriate to particular occasions of devotion; 3. Sacred Poems less intimately related to ecclesiastical services, selected from both Catholic and Protestant writers.

From the whole vast range of Christian thought, experience, and imagination, therefore,—from the fresh melodies lifted in the morning air of the Christian ages,—from that long line of consecrated and aspiring singers reaching back to the days of Constantine,—from among the lofty strains of Ambrose and Jerome and their strong fellow-believers, where the sanctity of centuries is so wrought, like an invisible aroma, into the very substance and structure of the verses, that it would seem as if some prophetic sense of their immortality had breathed in the men that wrote them,—from the secret cells and the high cathedrals of the Continental worship, where scholarship, and art, and power joined with piety to raise the Lauds and Glorias, the Matins and Vespers, the Sequences and the Choral Harmonies of a gorgeously appointed Praise,—from the purer literature of Old England, embracing the tender and earnest numbers of Southwell, and Crashaw, and Habington, and a multitude better known besides,—these voices of Faith are reverently gathered into their perfect harmony.

The volume is offered to the thoughtful portion of our community, with a cheerful confidence that it will fulfil an elevating, purifying, comforting ministry in many hearts, closets, and homes. Nor will its worth fail to be the more cordially confessed in many quarters, because so much in it favors the general tendency to recognize the observances and associations of the CHRISTIAN YEAR.

CAMBRIDGE, JUNE 1858. F. D. H.

EXTRACTS

From the Preface of EDWARD CASWALL, M. A., to his *Lyra Catholica.*

IT has been the object to exhibit for the firft time in an Englifh form, the entire series of those divine Hymns, which, in their Latin originals, have through ages been, and ftill continue to be, to countless saintly souls, the joy and consolation of their earthly pilgrimage.

" The present contribution to the exifting ftore of Catholic vernacular Hymns, confifts of three portions. The firft, and by far the largeft portion, comprehends all the Hymns in the Roman Breviary, including those in the Officia Sanctorum Angliæ; the second portion comprises the Hymns and Sequences of the Roman Miffal; and the third confifts of Hymns from various sources. Of these latter it may be observed, that the Hymns on the Nativity, Annunciation, and Vifitation, of our Bleffed Lady, as also those to St. Anne, St. Stephen, and St. John the Evangelift, are from the Monaftic Breviary of Cluny; those on the Purification and the Affumption, the Hymn to Jesus, and that for Sunday Morning, from the Parifian Breviary; and those to St. Joseph, St. Peter, St. Paul, and St. Pius the Fifth, from the *Raccolta delle Indulgenze.*

" As respects the Hymns in general, it may be useful to remark, that the greater number of them appear to have been originally written, not with a view to private reading, but for the purpose of being sung to the beautiful ecclefiaftical melodies by Monaftic and other Religious Bodies at their Office in Choir. This circumftance will serve to explain a few scattered expreffions, which otherwise might seem unreal ; as, for inftance, where allufions occur to the practice of rifing at midnight to fing praises to God ;—and if, on the one hand, some few of the Hymns may so far appear less adapted to the use of persons living in the world, it is our gain surely, on the other hand, thus, by occafional glimpses, to be reminded of that more perfect life, which has never ceased to be a reality in the Catholic Church.

" Another advantage, which we owe, doubtless, in a measure, to the same circumftance—an advantage not to be despised in a sentimental age—is the exceedingly plain and practical character of these Hymns. Written with a view to conftant daily use, they aim at something more than merely exciting the feelings. They have a perpetual reference to action. Their character is eminently objective. Their tendency is, to take the individual out of himself; to set before him, in turn, all the varied and sublime Objects of Faith ; and to blend him with the universal family of the Faithful.

" And here, although the Tranflator may seem to be pleading his own cause, yet he cannot refrain from observing, that truly poetical as are many of these Hymns, as indeed well befits the sacred outpourings of Chrift's tender Spouse, ftill, as a whole, the devotional is their primary and leaft disappointing aspect. Whoever attempts to read them as mere poetry, will obtain from them little of that delight which they are capable of inspiring. And as this is true of the original Latin, so it is truer ſtill of the Hymns as they appear in the present tranſlation; in which, it is to be feared, the unadorned ſimplicity of the prototype has too often degenerated into plainness; while its beauties have been faintly reflected, and their clear edge blunted in paſſing through a too earthly medium."

CONTENTS.

LYRA CATHOLICA
	PAGE
MATINS	3
VESPERS	19
ASPIRATION	23
SELF-CONSECRATION	29
TRUST	39
PRAYER	50
ENCOURAGEMENT	56
SELF-EXAMINATION	61
CHRIST	73
SAINTS, MARTYRS, &C	100
COMMUNION SERVICE	116
DEDICATION OF A CHURCH	119
MISCELLANEOUS	122

LYRA GERMANICA 137
LYRA APOSTOLICA 179
LYRA INNOCENTIUM 193
MISCELLANEOUS 215

LYRA CATHOLICA.

A

LYRA CATHOLICA.

MATINS.

O BLEST Creator of the light!
　Who doſt the dawn from darkness bring;
And framing Nature's depth and height,
　Didſt with the new-born light begin;

Who gently blending eve with morn,
　And morn with eve, didſt call them day:—
Thick flows the flood of darkness down;
　Oh, hear us as we weep and pray!

Keep thou our souls from schemes of crime;
　Nor guilt remorseful let them know;
Nor, thinking but on things of time,
　Into eternal darkness go.

Teach us to knock at Heaven's high door;
　Teach us the prize of life to win;
Teach us all evil to abhor,
　And purify ourselves within.
Breviary.

Matins.

NOW doth the sun ascend the sky,
   And wake creation with its ray;
Keep us from sin, O Lord most high!
   Through all the actions of the day.

Curb Thou for us th' unruly tongue;
   Teach us the way of peace to prize;
And close our eyes against the throng
   Of earth's absorbing vanities.

Oh, may our hearts be pure within!
   No cherish'd madness vex the soul!
May abstinence the flesh restrain,
   And its rebellious pride control.

So when the evening stars appear,
   And in their train the darkness bring;
May we, O Lord, with conscience clear,
   Our praise to thy pure glory sing.
                           Breviary.

Matins.

OUR limbs with tranquil sleep refresh'd
　　Lightly from bed we spring;
Father supreme! to us be nigh
　　While to thy praise we sing.

Thy love be first in every heart
　　Thy name on every tongue;
Whatever we this day may do,
　　May it in Thee be done.

Soon will the morning star arise,
　　And chase the dusk away;
Whatever guilt has come with night,
　　May it depart with day.

Cut off in us, Almighty Lord,
　　All that may lead to shame;
So with pure hearts may we in bliss
　　Thine endless praise proclaim.

　　　　　　　　Breviary.

GREAT Framer of the earth and sky,
Who doſt the light and darkness give!
And all the cheerful change supply
Of alternating morn and eve!

Light of the midnight traveller!
Who doſt divide the day from night!—
Loud crows the dawn's ſhrill harbinger,
And wakens up the sunbeams bright.

Forthwith at this, the darkness chill
Retreats before the ſtar of morn;
And from their busy schemes of ill,
The vagrant crews of night return.

Freſh hope, at this, the sailor cheers;
The waves their ſtormy ſtrife allay;
The Church's Rock at this, in tears,
Haſtens to waſh his guilt away.

Arise ye, then, with one accord!
Nor longer wrapt in ſlumber lie;
The cock rebukes all who their Lord
By ſloth negleƈt, by ſin deny.

Matins.

At his clear cry joy springs afreſh;
   Health courses through the sick man's veins;
The dagger glides into its ſheath;
   The fallen soul her faith regains.

Jesu! look on us when we fall;—
   One momentary glance of thine
Can from her guilt the soul recall
   To tears of penitence divine.

Awake us from false ſleep profound,
   And through our senses pour thy light;
Be thy bleſt name the firſt we sound
   At early dawn, the laſt at night.
Breviary.

COME, Holy Ghoſt, and through each heart
In thy full flood of glory pour;
Who, with the Son and Father, art
One Godhead bleſt for evermore.

So ſhall voice, mind, and ſtrength conspire
Thy praise eternal to resound;
So ſhall our hearts be set on fire,
And kindle every heart around.

Father of mercies! hear our cry;
Hear us, O sole-begotten Son!
Who, with the Holy Ghoſt moſt high,
Reigneſt while endless ages run.
Breviary.

LORD of eternal truth and might!
Ruler of nature's changing scheme!
Who doſt bring forth the morning light,
And temper noon's effulgent beam:

Quench Thou in us the flames of ſtrife,
And bid the heat of passion cease;
From perils guard our feeble life,
And keep our souls in perfeᣳ peace.
Breviary.

Rerum Deus tenax vigor.

O THOU true life of all that live!
    Who doft, unmoved, all motion sway;
Who doft the morn and evening give,
    And through its changes guide the day:

Thy light upon our evening pour,—
    So may our souls no sunset see;
But death to us an open door
    To an eternal morning be.

Father of mercies! hear our cry;
    Hear us, O sole-begotten Son!
Who, with the Holy Ghoft moft high,
    Reigneft while endless ages run.

Breviary.

LET us arise and watch ere dawn of light,
    And to the Lord our hearts and voices raise;
And meditate in psalms, and all unite
    In holy hymns of praise.

So joining in the ftrains of saints on high
Hereafter, in the courts of heaven's great King,
May we be meet his praise eternally
    With them in bliss to sing.

Breviary.

Matins.

O THOU the Father's Image bleſt!
Who calleſt forth the morning ray;
O Thou eternal Light of light!
And inexhauſtive Fount of day!

True Sun! upon our souls arise,
　Shining in beauty evermore;
And through each sense the quick'ning beam
　Of the eternal Spirit pour.

Thee too, O Father, we entreat,
　Father of might and grace divine!
Father of glorious majeſty!
　Thy pitying eye on us incline.

Confirm us in each good resolve;
　The Tempter's envious rage subdue;
Turn each misfortune to our good;
　Direct us right in all we do.

Rule Thou our inmoſt thoughts; let no
　Impurity our hearts defile;
Grant us a true and fervent faith;
　Grant us a spirit free from guile.

May Chriſt himself be our true Food,
　And Faith our daily cup supply;

While from the Spirit's tranquil depth
　　We drink unfailing draughts of joy.

Still ever with the peep of morn
　　May saintly modefty attend;
Faith sanctify the midday hours;
　　Upon the soul no night descend.

Faſt breaks the dawn.—Each whole in Each,
　　Come, Father bleſt! Come, Son moſt high!
Shine in our souls, and be to them
　　The dawn of immortality.
　　　　　　　　　　　　Breviary.

———◆———

LO, fainter now lie spread the shades of night,
　　And upward ſhoot the trembling gleams of morn;
Suppliant we bend before the Lord of Light,
　　And pray at early dawn,—

That his sweet charity may all our ſin
Forgive, and make our miseries to cease;
May grant us health, grant us the gift divine
　　Of everlaſting peace.
　　　　　　　　　　　　Breviary.

THE CHRISTIAN TO HIS SOUL AT SUNRISE.

SOIL not thy plumage, gentle dove,
   With sublunary things,—
Till in the fount of light and love,
   Thou fhalt have bathed thy wings.

Shall Nature from her couch arise,
   And rise for thee in vain?
While heaven, and earth, and seas, and fkies,
   Such types of truth contain.

See—where the Sun of Righteousness,
   Unfolds the gates of day:
Go,—meet Him in his glorious dress,
   And quaff the orient ray!

There, where ten thousand seraphs ftand,
   To crown the circling hours,—
Soar thou,—and from that blifsful land
   Bring down unfading flowers:

Some Rose of Sharon, dyed in blood,
   Some spice of Gilead's balm,
Some lily wafhed in Calvary's flood,
   Some branch of heavenly palm!

And let the drops of sparkling dew,
   From Siloa's spring be fhed,

To form a fragrance freſh and new,
    A halo round thy head.

Spread then thy plumes of faith and prayer,
    Nor fear to wend away;
And let a glow of heavenly air,
    Gild every earthly day!
Brydges.

Consors paterni luminis.

PURE Light of light! eternal Day!
    Who doſt the Father's brightness ſhare;
Our chant the midnight silence breaks;—
    Be nigh, and hearken to our prayer.

Scatter the darkness of our minds,
    And turn the hoſts of hell to flight;
Let not our souls in ſloth repose,
    And ſleeping ſink in endless night.

O Chriſt! for thy dear mercy's sake,
    Spare us, who put our truſt in Thee;
Nor let our hymns ascend in vain
    To thy immortal Majesty.
Breviary.

NOW, while the herald bird of day
  Proclaims the morning bright;
Chrift also, speaking in the soul,
  Wakes her to life and light.

"Take up your beds," we hear Him say,
  "No more in flumber lie;
In juftice, truth, and temperance,
  Keep watch;—Your Lord is nigh."

O Chrift! and art Thou nigh indeed?—
  Then let us watch and weep;
This truth but once in earneft felt
  Forbids the heart to fleep.

Break, Lord, the spell that wraps us round
  In deadly bonds of night;
Shatter the chains of former guilt;
  Renew in us thy light.
                              Breviary.

Nox et tenebræ et nubila.

YE mist and darkness, cloud and storm,
   Confused creations of the night;
Light enters—morning streaks the sky—
   Christ comes,—'tis time ye take your flight.

Pierced by the sun's ethereal dart,
   Night's gloomy mass is cleft in twain;
And, in the smiling face of day,
   Nature resumes her tints again.

O God, we know no sun but Thee!
   Shine in our souls divinely bright!
We seek Thee in simplicity;
   Through all our senses shed thy light.

A thousand objects all around
   In false delusive colors shine;
To purge them clear, we ask, O Lord,
   But one immortal beam of thine.
                               Breviary.

Lux ecce surgit aurea.

NOW with the rising golden dawn,
    Let us, the children of the day,
Cast off the darkness which so long
    Has led our guilty souls astray.

Oh, may the morn so pure, so clear,
    Its own sweet calm in us instil;
A guileless mind, a heart sincere,
    Simplicity of word and will:

And ever, as the day glides by,
    May we the busy senses rein;
Keep guard upon the hand and eye,
    Nor let the body suffer stain.

For all day long, on Heaven's high tower,
    There stands a Sentinel, who spies
Our every action, hour by hour,
    From early dawn till daylight dies.
                                    Breviary.

Matins.

GRANT us a body pure within;
  A wakeful heart, a ready will;
Grant us, by no deep cherish'd sin,
  The fervor of the soul to chill.

Fill Thou our souls, Redeemer true!
  With thy most pure celestial ray;
So may we walk in safety through
  All the temptations of this day.
      Breviary.

UPON our fainting souls distil
  The grace of thy celestial dew;
Let no fresh snare to sin beguile,
  No former sin revive anew.

Grant us the grace, for love of Thee,
  To scorn all vanities below;
Faith to detect each falsity;
  And knowledge, Thee alone to know.
      Breviary.

THE ſtar that heralds in the morn
　　Is fading in the ſkies;
The darkness melts;—O Thou true Light!
　　Upon our souls arise.

Steep all our senses in' thy beam;
　　The world's false night expel;
Purge each defilement from the soul,
　　And in our bosoms dwell.

Come, early Faith! fix in our hearts
　　Thy root immovably;
Come, smiling Hope! and, laſt not leaſt,
　　Immortal Charity!

Breviary.

VESPERS.

CHRISTMAS VESPER HYMN.

DEPART awhile, each thought of care,
    Be earthly things forgotten all;
And speak, my soul, thy vesper prayer;
    Obedient to that sacred call.
For hark! the pealing chorus swells;
    Devotion chants the hymn of praise,
And now of joy and hope it tells,
    Till fainting on the ear, it says—
        Gloria tibi Domine,
          Domine, Domine.

Thine, wondrous babe of Galilee!
    Fond theme of David's harp and song,
Thine are the notes of minftrelsy—
    To thee its ransom'd chords belong.
And hark! again the chorus swells,
    The song is wafted on the breeze,
And to the liftening earth it tells—
    In accents soft and sweet as these—
        Gloria tibi Domine.

My heart doth feel that ſtill He's near,
  To meet the soul in hours like this,
Else—why, O why, that falling tear!
  When all is peace and love and bliss!
But hark! that pealing chorus swells
  Anew, its thrilling vesper ſtrain,
And ſtill of joy and hope it tells,
  And bids creation ſing again—
    Gloria tibi Domine.

J. Hughes.

COME, O Creator Spirit bleſt!
  And in our souls take up thy reſt;
Come, with thy grace and heavenly aid,
To fill the hearts which Thou haſt made.

Kindle our senses from above,
And make our hearts o'erflow with love;
With patience firm, and virtue high,
The weakness of our fleſh supply.

Far from us drive the foe we dread,
And grant us thy true peace inſtead;
So ſhall we not, with Thee for guide,
Turn from the path of life aſide.

Breviary.

THE pall of night o'erſhades the earth,
    And hides the tints of day;—
O Thou! to whom no night comes near,
    Dread Judge! to Thee we pray!

That Thou wilt all our guilt remove,
    And our loſt peace reſtore;
And of thy mercy grant that we
    May grieve thy heart no more.

The guilty soul, which all too long
    In lethargy hath lain,
Yearns to caſt off her load, and seek
    Her Saviour's face again.

Expel from her the darkness, Lord,
    Of her internal night;
Renew her bliss,—renew in her
    Thy beatific light.

Breviary.

LORD of eternal purity!
Who doſt the world with light adorn,
And paint the tracts of azure ſky
　With lovely hues of eve and morn:

Who didſt command the sun to light
　His fiery wheel's effulgent blaze;
Didſt set the moon her circuit bright;
　The ſtars their ever-winding maze:

That, each within its order'd sphere,
　They might divide the night from day;
And of the seasons through the year,
　The well remember'd signs display:

Scatter our night, eternal God,
　And kindle thy pure beam within;
Free us from guilt's oppreſſive load,
　And break the deadly bonds of ſin.
　　　　　　　　　　　　Breviary.

———◆———

THEE in the hymns of morn we praise;
To Thee our voice at eve we raise;
Oh, grant us, with thy Saints on high,
Thee through all time to glorify.
　　　　　　　　　　　　Breviary.

ASPIRATION.

PERFECTION.

O HOW the thought of God attracts
    And draws the heart from earth,
And sickens it of passing shows
    And dissipating mirth!

'Tis not enough to save our souls,
    To shun the eternal fires;
The thought of God will rouse the heart
    To more sublime desires.

God only is the creature's home,
    Though long and rough the road;
Yet nothing less can satisfy
    The love that longs for God.

O utter but the Name of God
    Down in your heart of hearts,
And see how from the world at once
    All tempting light departs.

A trusting heart, a yearning eye,
  Can win their way above;
If mountains can be moved by faith,
  Is there less power in love?

How little of that road, my soul!
  How little hast thou gone!
Take heart, and let the thought of God
  Allure thee further on.

The freedom from all wilful sin,
  The Christian's daily task,—
O these are graces far below
  What longing love would ask!

Dole not thy duties out to God,
  But let thy hand be free:
Look long at Jesus; his sweet Blood,
  How was it dealt to thee?

The perfect way is hard to flesh;
  It is not hard to love;
If thou wert sick for want of God,
  How swiftly wouldst thou move!

Good is the cloister's silent shade,
  Cold watch and pining fast;
Better the missions wearing strife,
  If there thy lot be cast.

Aspiration.

Yet none of these perfection needs :—
   Keep thy heart calm all day,
And catch the words the Spirit there
   From hour to hour may say.

O keep thy conscience senfitive ;
   No inward token miss ;
And go where grace entices thee ;—
   Perfection lies in this.

Be docile to thine unseen Guide,
   Love Him as He loves thee ;
Time and obedience are enough,
   And thou a saint shalt be !

Faber.

THE ETERNAL FATHER.

O HOW I fear Thee, living God!
    With deepeſt, tendereſt fears,
And worſhip Thee with trembling hope,
    And penitential tears.

Yet I may love Thee too, O Lord!
    Almighty as Thou art,
For Thou haſt ſtooped to aſk of me
    The love of my poor heart.

O then this worse than worthless heart
    In pity deign to take,
And make it love Thee for thyself
    And for thy glory's sake.

No earthly father loves like Thee,
    No mother half so mild
Bears and forbears, as Thou haſt done,
    With me thy ſinful child.

Only to ſit and think of God—
    O what a joy it is!
To think the thought, to breathe the Name—
    Earth has no higher bliss!

Aspiration.

Father of Jesus! love's Reward!
What rapture will it be
Proſtrate before thy throne to lie,
And gaze and gaze on Thee!
Faber.

PECCATOR AD CHRISTUM.

MY spirit longeth for Thee
To dwell within my breaſt;
Although I am unworthy
Of so divine a Gueſt!

Of so divine a Gueſt—
Unworthy though I be;
Yet hath my heart no reſt
Until it come to Thee!

Until it come to Thee,—
In vain I look around;
In all that I can see,
No rest is to be found!

No reſt is to be found,
But in thy bleeding love:
Oh! let my wiſh be crown'd,
And send it from above!
Brydges.

CHRISTUS AD PECCATOREM.

CHEER up, desponding soul,
   Thy longing pleased I see:
'Tis part of that great whole,
   Wherewith I long'd for thee!

Wherewith I long'd for thee,
   And left my Father's throne;
From death to set thee free,
   And claim thee for my own!

To claim thee for my own,
   I suffer'd on the cross:
Oh! were my love but known,
   All else would be as dross!

All else would be as dross!
   And souls, through grace divine,
Would count their gains but loss,
   To live forever mine!

Brydges.

SELF-CONSECRATION.

FAITH OF OUR FATHERS.

FAITH of our Fathers! living ſtill
    In ſpite of dungeon, fire, and sword:
Oh how our hearts beat high with joy
    Whene'er we hear that glorious word:
Faith of our Fathers! Holy Faith!
We will be true to thee till death!

Our Fathers, chain'd in prisons dark,
    Were ſtill in heart and conscience free:
How sweet would be their children's fate,
    If they, like them, could die for thee!
Faith of our Fathers! Holy Faith!
We will be true to thee till death!

Faith of our Fathers! we will love
    Both friend and foe in all our ſtrife:
And preach thee too, as love knows how
    By kindly words and virtuous life:
Faith of our Fathers! Holy Faith!
We will be true to thee till death!

Faber.

THE VOW.

BRIGHT Angels who attend
    Around our altar now,
Your wonted cares suspend,
    Lift to the holy Vow,
Which, while the sacrifice
    Of Heaven's eternal love,
Pleads for us every grace,
    Is heard in heaven above.

Jesus! my happy heart
    Now gives itself to Thee,
O! never hence depart,
    Reign here eternally.
Thy sacred name alone,
    All my delight shall prove;
No joy my soul shall own,
    But in thy holy love.

And, oh! in after years,
    When life is fading fast,
When flow repentant tears,
    Cancelling errors past,
Still shall that holy vow,
    Be breathed to Heaven,
And fervently as now,
    My heart to Thee be given.

HYMN FOR CONFIRMATION.

MY God, accept my heart this day,
    And make it always thine,—
That I from Thee no more may ſtray,
    No more from Thee decline.

Before the cross of Him who died,
    Behold I proſtrate fall:
Let every ſin be crucified,—
    Let Chriſt be all in all!

Anoint me with thy heavenly grace,
    Adopt me for thine own,—
That I may see thy glorious face,
    And worſhip at thy throne!

May the dear blood, once ſhed for me,
    My bleſt atonement prove,—
That I from firſt to laſt may be
    The purchase of thy love!

Let every thought, and work, and word, *[wish]*
    To Thee be ever given,—
Then life ſhall be thy service, Lord,
    And death the gate of heaven.

                            Brydges.

JESUS, I MY CROSS HAVE TAKEN.

Crux sublata. Matt. xvi. 24.

JESUS,—I my cross have taken,
 All to leave and follow Thee;
I am poor, despised, forsaken,—
 Thou henceforth my all shalt be:
Perish every fond ambition,—
 All I've sought, or hoped, or known;
Yet how rich is my condition,—
 God and heaven are still mine own!

Let the world despise and leave me,
 It has left my Saviour too;
Human hearts and looks deceive me,
 Thou art not like them untrue:
Whilst thy graces shall adorn me,
 God of wisdom, love, and might,—
Foes may hate, and friends may scorn me;—
 Show thy face, and all is bright.

Go then,—earthly fame and treasure,
 Come, disaster, scorn, and pain;
In thy service, pain is pleasure,—
 With thy favor, loss is gain.
I have called Thee, Abba Father!
 I have set my heart on Thee:

Storms may howl, and clouds may gather,
    All will work for good to me.

Man may trouble and diftress me,
    'Twill but drive me to thy breaft;
Life with trials hard may press me
    Heaven will bring me sweeter reft.
Oh, 'tis not in grief to harm me
    While thy love is left to me;—
Oh, 'twere not in joy to charm me,
    Were that joy unmixed with Thee!

Soul,—then know thy full salvation,
    Rise o'er fin, and fear, and care;
Joy to find in every ftation,
    Something ftill to do or bear.
Think what spirit dwells within thee,
    Think what Father's smiles are thine;
Think that Jesus died to win thee:
    Child of heaven, cans't thou repine?

Hafte thee on from grace to glory,
    Armed by faith, and winged by prayer,—
Heaven's eternal days before thee,
    God's own hand fhall guide thee there.
Soon fhall close thine earthly miffion,
    Patience fhall thy spirit raise;
Hope fhall change to glad fruition,
    Faith to sight, and prayer to praise!

CONVERSION.

O FAITH! thou workeft miracles
Upon the hearts of men,
Choofing thy home in those same hearts,
We know not how or when.

To one thy grave unearthly truths
A heavenly vifion seem;
While to another's eye they are
A superftitious dream.

To one the deepeft doctrines look
So naturally true,
That when he learns the leffon firft
He hardly thinks it new.

To other hearts the selfsame truths
No light or heat can bring;
They are but puzzling phrases ftrung
Like beads upon a ftring.

O Gift of Gifts! O Grace of Faith!
My God! how can it be
That Thou, who haft discerning love,
Should'ft give that gift to me?

Self-Consecration. 35

There was a place, there was a time,
    Whether by night or day,
Thy Spirit came and left that gift,
    And went upon his way.

How many hearts Thou might'st have had
    More innocent than mine!
How many souls more worthy far
    Of that sweet touch of thine!

Ah Grace! into unlikeliest hearts
    It is thy boast to come,
The glory of thy light to find
    In darkest spots a home.

How will they die, how will they die,
    How bear the cross of grief,
Who have not got the light of faith,
    The courage of belief?

The crowd of cares, the weightiest cross
    Seem trifles less than light,—
Earth looks so little and so low
    When faith shines full and bright.

O happy, happy that I am!
    If thou canst be, O Faith!
The treasure that thou art in life,
    What wilt thou be in death?

Thy choice, O God of Goodness! then
  I lovingly adore;
O give me grace to keep thy grace,
  And grace to merit more!

Faber.

PRAYER OF THE CONTRITE SINNER.

HAVE mercy Thou, moſt gracious God!
  And my remittance ſign;
The more thy mercy ſhall accord,
  The greater glory thine.

Thou surely haſt not said in vain:
  " More joy in heaven is made,
For the loſt ſheep that's found again,
  Than those which never stray'd."

Help'd by thy grace, no more I'll stray,
  No more refiſt thy voice;
Where Thou, good Shepherd, lead'ſt the way,
  That way ſhall be my choice.

Too long, alas! my wand'ring feet
  The crooked paths have trod;
Henceforth I'll follow, as is meet,
  The sure unerring road.

Self-Consecration.

If casual falls retard my pace,
  With speed again I'll rise;
With speed I'll reassume my race,
  And run and gain the prize.

All praise, O Lord, to Thee alone,
  Below, as 'tis above :
And may thy joys, Eternal One,
  Both draw and crown my love.

HYMN OF ST. FRANCIS XAVIER.

O Deus, ego amo Te.

MY God, I love Thee, not because
  I hope for Heaven thereby;
Nor because they who love Thee not,
  Must burn eternally.

Thou, O my Jesus, Thou didft me
  Upon the Cross embrace;
For me didft bear the nails and spear,
  And manifold disgrace;

And griefs and torments numberless;
  And sweat of agony;
E'en death itself—and all for one
  Who was thine enemy.

Self-Consecration.

Then why, O bleſſed Jesu Chriſt!
  Should I not love Thee well;
Not for the sake of winning Heaven,
  Or of escaping Hell:

Not with the hope of gaining aught;
  Not seeking a reward;
But, as Thyself haſt loved me,
  O ever-loving Lord?

E'en so I love Thee, and will love,
  And in thy praise will ſing;
Solely because Thou art my God,
  And my eternal King.

Missal.

TRUST.

THE RIGHT MUST WIN.

O IT is hard to work for God,
    To rise and take his part
Upon this battle-field of earth,
    And not sometimes lose heart!

He hides Himself so wondroufly,
    As though there were no God;
He is leaft seen when all the powers
    Of ill are moft abroad:

Or He deserts us at the hour
    The fight is all but loft;
And seems to leave us to ourselves
    Juft when we need Him moft.

O there is less to try our faith,
    In our myfterious creed,
Than in the godless look of earth
    In these our hours of need.

Ill mafters good; good seems to change
To ill with greateft ease;
And, worft of all, the good with good
Is at cross purposes.

The Church, the Sacraments, the Faith,
Their uphill journey take,
Lose here what there they gain, and, if
We lean upon them, break.

It is not so, but so it looks;
And we lose courage then;
And doubts will come if God hath kept
His promises to men.

Ah! God is other than we think;
His ways are far above,
Far beyond reason's height, and reach'd
Only by childlike love.

The look, the fafhion of God's ways
Love's lifelong ftudy are;
She can be bold, and guess, and act,
When reason would not dare.

She has a prudence of her own;
Her ftep is firm and free;
Yet there is cautious science too
In her simplicity.

Workman of God! O lose not heart,
    But learn what God is like;
And in the darkeſt battle-field
    Thou ſhalt know where to ſtrike.

O bleſs'd is he to whom is given
    The inſtinct that can tell
That God is on the field, when He
    Is moſt invisible!

And bleſs'd is he who can divine
    Where real right doth lie,
And dares to take the side that seems
    Wrong to man's blindfold eye!

O learn to scorn the praise of men!
    O learn to lose with God!
For Jesus won the world through ſhame,
    And beckons thee his road.

God's glory is a wondrous thing,
    Moſt ſtrange in all its ways,
And, of all things on earth, leaſt like
    What men agree to praise.

As He can endless glory weave
    From time's misjudging shame,
In his own world He is content
    To play a loſing game.

Muse on his juftice, downcaft Soul!
  Muse and take better heart;
Back with thine angel to the field,
  Good luck fhall crown thy part!

God's juftice is a bed where we
  Our anxious hearts may lay,
And, weary with ourselves, may sleep
  Our discontent away.

For right is right, since God is God;
  And right the day muft win;
To doubt would be disloyalty,
  To falter would be sin!

Faber.

SURSUM CORDA.

"LIFT up your hearts!" Yes, I will lift
    My heart and soul, dear Lord, to Thee
Who every good and perfect gift
    Vouchsaf'st so lavishly and free.

All that is best, from Thee comes down
    On us, with rich and ample store,
Thy bounteous hands our wishes crown
    With good, increasing more and more.

'Twas Thou that gave us life and breath,
    It is thy hand that holds us still,
That keeps us from the sleep of death,
    And shelters us from every ill.

Yea, more than corporal life,—thy love
    Has promise given of life to come;
And taught us, by the faith, above
    All ills to soar, and burst the tomb.

Then, while I live, with ardent eye,
    Let me look up to Thee, and learn,
From blessings *here*, to look on high,
    And purer blessings *there* discern!

All Thou haſt given is thine, then take
  Me, thine own gift, for all thine own,
And teach me every day to make
  New vows of love to Thee alone!

GOD AND HEAVEN.

THE silver chord in twain is snapp'd
    The golden bowl is broken,
The mortal mould in darkness wrapp'd,
    The words funereal spoken;
The tomb is built, or the rock is cleft,
    Or delved is the graſſy clod,
And what for mourning man is left?
    O what is left—but God!

The tears are ſhed that mourn'd the dead,
    The flowers they wore are faded;
The twilight dun hath veil'd the sun,
    And hope's sweet dreamings ſhaded:
And the thoughts of joy that were planted deep,
    From our heart of hearts are riven;
And what is left us when we weep?
    O what is left—but Heaven!

THE WILL OF GOD.

" Thy will be done."

I WORSHIP thee, sweet Will of God!
    And all thy ways adore,
And every day I live I seem
    To love thee more and more.

Thou wert the end, the bleffed rule
    Of Jesu's toils and tears;
Thou wert the paffion of his Heart
    Those Three-and-Thirty years.

And He hath breathed into my soul
    A spécial love of thee,
A love to lose my will in his
    And by that loss be free.

I love to see thee bring to naught
    The plans of wily men;
When fimple Hearts outwit the wise,
    O thou art loveliest then!

The headftrong world, it preffes hard
    Upon the Church full oft,
And then how eafily thou turn'ft
    The hard ways into soft.

I love to kiss each print where thou
　Haſt set thine unseen feet :
I cannot fear thee, bleſſed Will!
　Thine empire is so sweet.

When obſtacles and trials seem
　Like prison-walls to be,
I do the little I can do,
　And leave the reſt to thee.

I have no cares, O bleſſed Will!
　For all my cares are thine ;
I live in triumph, Lord! for Thou
　Haſt made thy triumphs mine.

And when it seems no chance or change
　From grief can set me free,
Hope finds its ſtrength in helpleſſneſs,
　And gaily waits on thee.

Man's weakness waiting upon God
　Its end can never miss,
For men on earth no work can do
　More angel-like than this.

Ride on, ride on triumphantly,
　Thou glorious Will! ride on ;
Faith's pilgrim sons behind thee take
　The road that thou haſt gone.

Trust.

He always wins who sides with God,
    To him no chance is loſt;
God's will is sweetest to him when
    It triumphs at his coſt.

Ill that He bleſſes is our good,
    And unbleſt good is ill;
And all is right that seems moſt wrong,
    If it be His sweet Will!

Faber.

Dies iræ, dies illa.

[Crashaw's Translation.]

HEAR'ST thou, my soul, what serious things
    Both the Psalm and Sibyl ſings,
Of a sure Judge, from whose ſharp ray
The world in flames ſhall pass away?

O that fire! before whose face,
Heaven and Earth ſhall find no place;
O these eyes! whose angry light
Muſt be the day of that dread night.

O that trump! whose blaſt ſhall run
An even round with th' circling sun,
And urge the murmuring graves to bring
Pale mankind forth to meet his King.

Horror of nature, hell and death!
When a deep groan as from beneath
Shall cry, "We come! we come!" and all
The caves of night answer one call.

O that book! whose leaves so bright,
Will set the world in severe light:
O that Judge! whose hand, whose eye,
None can endure—yet none can fly.

Ah! thou poor soul, what wilt thou say?
And to what patron choose to pray?
When ſtars themselves ſhall ſtagger, and
The moſt firm foot no more than ſtand.

But thou giveſt leave, dread Lord, that we
Take ſhelter from Thyself in Thee;
And, with the wings of thine own dove,
Fly to the sceptre of soft love.

MY GOD AND MY ALL.

Deus meus et omnia.

WHILE Thou, O my God, art my help and defender,
   No cares can o'erwhelm me, no terrors appall;
The wiles and the snares of this world will but render
   More lively my hope in my God and my all.

Yes; Thou art my refuge in sorrow and danger;
   My ſtrength when I suffer; my hope when I fall;
My comfort and joy in this land of the ſtranger;
   My treasure, my glory, my God, and my all.

To Thee, deareſt Lord, will I turn without ceaſing,
   Though grief may oppress me, or sorrow befall;
And love Thee, till death, my bleſt spirit releaſing,
   Secures to me Jesus, my God and my all.

And when Thou demandeſt the life Thou haſt given,
   With joy will I answer thy merciful call;
And quit Thee on earth, but to find Thee in heaven,
   My portion forever, my God and my all.

W. Young.

PRAYER.

Telluris alme conditor.

O BOUNTEOUS Framer of the globe!
   Who with thy mighty hand
Didſt gather up the rolling seas,
   And firmly base the land:

That so the freſhly teeming earth
   Might herb and seedling bear,
Standing in early beauty gay,
   With flowers and fruitage fair:

On our parch'd souls pour Thou, O Lord,
   The freſhness of thy grace;
So penitence ſhall spring anew,
   And all the paſt efface.

Grant us to fear thy holy law,
   To feel thy goodness nigh;
Grant us through life thy peace; in death
   Thine immortality.
                          Breviary.

WHIT-SUNDAY.

Veni Sancte Spiritus.

HOLY Spirit! Lord of light!
From thy clear celeftial height,
  Thy pure beaming radiance give:

Come, Thou Father of the poor!
Come, with treasures which endure!
  Come, Thou Light of all that live;

Thou, of all consolers beft,
Vifiting the troubled breaft,
  Doft refrefhing peace beftow;

Thou in toil art comfort sweet;
Pleasant coolness in the heat;
  Solace in the midft of woe.

Light immortal! light divine!
Vifit Thou these hearts of thine,
  And our inmoft being fill:

If Thou take thy grace away,
Nothing pure in man will ftay;
  All his good is turned to ill.

Heal our wounds,—our strength renew;
On our dryness pour thy dew;
  Wash the stains of guilt away:

Bend the stubborn heart and will;
Melt the frozen, warm the chill;
  Guide the steps that go astray.

Thou, on those who evermore
Thee confess and Thee adore,
  In thy sevenfold gifts, descend:

Give them comfort when they die;
Give them life with Thee on high;
  Give them joys which never end.
                                    Missal.

Veni Creator.

CREATOR Spirit, by whose aid
  The world's foundations first were laid,
Come visit every pious mind;
Come pour thy joys on human kind;
From sin and sorrow set us free
And make thy temples worthy Thee.

O source of uncreated light
The Father's promised Paraclete!

Prayer.

Thrice holy fount, thrice holy fire,
Our hearts with heavenly love inspire:
Come, and thy sacred unction bring,
To sanctify us while we sing.

Plenteous of grace, descend from high,
Rich in thy sevenfold energy!
Thou strength of his Almighty hand,
Whose power does heaven and earth command,
Proceeding Spirit, our defence,
Who dost the gift of tongues dispense,
And crown thy gift with eloquence!

Refine and purge our earthly parts:
But oh! inflame and fire our hearts:
Our frailties help, our vice control—
Submit the senses to the soul:
And when rebellious they are grown,
Then lay thy hand, and hold them down.

Chase from our minds th' infernal foe,
And peace, the fruit of love, bestow;
And lest our feet should step astray,
Protect and guide us in the way.

Make us eternal truth receive,
And practise all that we believe:
Give us Thyself, that we may see
The Father, and the Son, by Thee.

Translated by Dryden.

LENT.

Audi benigne Conditor.

THOU loving Maker of mankind,
   Before thy throne we pray and weep;
Oh, ftrengthen us with grace divine,
   Duly this sacred Lent to keep.

Searcher of hearts! Thou doft our ills
   Discern, and all our weakness know:
Again to Thee with tears we turn;
   Again to us thy mercy fhow.

Much have we finn'd; but we confess
   Our guilt, and all our faults deplore:
Oh, for the praise of thy great Name,
   Our fainting souls to health reftore!

And grant us, while by fafts we ftrive
   This mortal body to control,
To faft from all the food of fin,
   And so to purify the soul.

Hear us, O Trinity thrice bleft!
   Sole Unity! to Thee we cry:
Vouchsafe us from these fafts below
   To reap immortal fruit on high.
                                Breviary.

Magnæ Deus potentiæ.

LORD of all power! at whose command,
  The waters, from their teeming womb,
Brought forth the countless tribes of fish,
  And birds of every note and plume:

Who didst, for natures link'd in birth,
  Far different homes of old prepare;
Sinking the fishes in the sea;
  Lifting the birds aloft in air.

Lo! born of thy baptismal wave,
  We ask of Thee, O Lord divine!
"Keep us, whom Thou hast sanctified
  In thy own Blood, forever thine.

"Safe from all pride, as from despair;
  Not sunk too low, nor raised too high
Lest raised by pride, we headlong fall;
  Sunk in despair, lie down and die."

Breviary.

ENCOURAGEMENT.

JESUS.

THE light of love is round his feet,
   His paths are never dim;
And He comes nigh to us when we
   Dare not come nigh to Him.

Let us be simple with Him then,
   Not backward, ftiff, or cold,
As though our Bethlehem could be
   What Sinai was of old.

His love of us may teach us how
   To love Him in return;
Love cannot help but grow more free
   The more its transports burn.

The solemn face, the downcaft eye,
   The words conftrain'd and cold,—
These are the homage, poor at beft,
   Of those outfide the fold.

Encouragement.

O that they knew what Jesus was,
    And what untold abyss
Lies in love's simple forwardness
    Of more than earthly bliss!

O that they knew what faith can work!
    What Sacraments can do!
What simple love is like, on fire
    In hearts absolved and true!

How can they tell but Jesus oft
    His secret thirst will slake,
On those strange freedoms childlike hearts
    Are taught by God to take?

Poor souls! they know not how to love;
    They feel not Jesus near;
And they who know not how to love
    Still less know how to fear.

The humbling of the Incarnate Word
    They have not faith to face;
And how shall they who have not faith
    Attain love's better grace?

The awe that lies too deep for words,
    Too deep for solemn looks,—
It finds no way into the face,
    No spoken vent in books.

They would not speak in measured tones,
   If love had in them wrought
Until their spirits had been hush'd
   In reverential thought.

They would have smiled in playful ways
   To ease their fervid heart,
And learn'd with other simple souls
   To play love's crafty part.

They would have run away from God
   For their own vileness' sake,
And fear'd left some interior light
   From tell-tale eyes should break.

They know not how the outward smile
   The inward awe can prove;
They fathom not the creature's fear
   Of Uncreated Love.

The majesty of God ne'er broke
   On them like fire at night,
Flooding their stricken souls, while they
   Lay trembling in the light.

They love not; for they have not kiss'd
   The Saviour's outer hem:
They fear not; for the Living God
   Is yet unknown to them!

Faber.

SOLDIERS of Christ! arise!
   And put your armor on,
Strong in the strength which God supplies
   Through his eternal Son;
Strong is the Lord of hosts,
   And in his mighty power,
Who in the strength of Jesus trusts,
   Is more than conqueror.

Soldiers of Christ! arise!
   The God of armies calls
Unto his mansions in the skies—
   His everlasting halls:
Behold! the angel host appears
   To welcome you to bliss;
Oh! what is earth, its sighs, and tears,
   Its joys compared to this!

Crush'd is the haughty foe,
   His might, his glory gone,
But ye with victory crown'd, shall go
   To Christ's eternal throne.
There shall the conqueror rest,
   And in that blest abode,
Forever reign amid the blest,
   Triumphant with his God.

MARY MAGDALEN.

TO the hall of the feaſt came the ſinful and fair;
She heard in the city that Jesus was there;
She mark'd not the splendor that blazed on their board;
But ſilently knelt at the feet of her Lord.

The hair from her forehead, so sad and so meek,
Hung dark o'er the blushes that burn'd on her cheek;
And so ſtill and so lowly ſhe bent in her ſhame,
It seem'd as her spirit had flown from its frame.

The frown and the murmur went round through them all,
That one so unhallow'd ſhould tread in that hall;
And some said the poor would be objects more meet
For the wealth of the perfumes ſhe ſhower'd at his feet.

She mark'd but her Saviour, ſhe spoke but in ſighs,
She dared not look up to the heaven of his eyes;
And the hot tears guſh'd forth at each heave of her breaſt,
As her lips to his sandals ſhe throbbingly preſſ'd.

On the cloud, after tempeſts, as ſhineth the bow,
In the glance of the sun-beam, as melteth the snow,
He look'd on that loſt one—her ſins were forgiven;
And Mary went forth in the beauty of heaven.

Callanan.

SELF-EXAMINATION.

THE GIFTS OF GOD.

MY soul! what haſt thou done for God?
　　Look o'er thy miſſpent years and see;
Sum up what thou haſt done for God,
　　And then what God hath done for thee.

He made thee when He might have made
　　A soul that would have loved Him more;
He rescued thee from nothingness,
　　And set thee on life's happy ſhore.

He placed an angel at thy ſide,
　　And ſtrewed joys round thee on thy way;
He gave thee rights thou couldſt not claim,
　　And life, free life, before thee lay.

Had God in heaven no work to do
　　But miracles of love for thee?
No world to rule, no joy in Self
　　And in his own infinity?

So must it seem to our blind eyes:
  He gave his love no Sabbath rest,
Still plotting happiness for men,
  And new designs to make them blest.

From out his glorious Bosom came
  His only, his Eternal Son;
He freed the race of Satan's slaves,
  And with his Blood sin's captives won.

The world rose up against his love;
  New love the vile rebellion met,
As though God only look'd at sin
  Its guilt to pardon and forget.

For his Eternal Spirit came
  To raise the thankless slaves to sons,
And with the sevenfold gifts of love
  To crown his own elected ones.

Men spurned his grace; their lips blasphemed
  The love that made itself their slave:
They grieved that blessed Comforter,
  And turned against Him what He gave.

Yet still the sun is fair by day,
  The moon still beautiful by night;
The world goes round, and joy with it,
  And life, free life, is man's delight.

Self-Examination.

No voice God's wondrous filence breaks,
   No hand put forth his anger tells ;
But He, the Omnipotent and Dread,
   On high in humbleft patience dwells.

The Son hath come; and maddened fin
   The world's Redeemer crucified ;
The Spirit comes, and ftays, while men
   His presence doubt, his gifts deride.

And now the Father keeps Himself
   In patient and forbearing love,
To be his creature's heritage
   In that undying life above.

O wonderful, O paffing thought,
   The love that God hath had for thee !
Spending on thee no less a sum
   Than the Undivided Trinity !

Father, and Son, and Holy Ghoft,
   Exhaufted for a thing like this,—
The world's whole government disposed
   For one ungrateful creature's bliss !

What haft thou done for God, my soul?
   Look o'er thy miffpent years and see ;
Cry from thy worse than nothingness,
   Cry for his mercy upon thee !
                         Faber.

SWEETNESS IN PRAYER.

WHY doſt thou beat so quick, my heart?
    Why ſtruggle in thy cage?
What ſhall I do for thee, poor heart!
    Thy throbbing heat to suage?

What spell is this come over thee?
    My soul! what sweet surprise?
And wherefore these unbidden tears
    That ſtart into mine eyes?

How are my paſſions laid to ſleep,
    How easy penance seems!
And how the bright world fades away—
    O are they all but dreams?

How great, how good does God appear,
    How dear our holy faith!
How taſteless life's beſt joys have grown!
    How I could welcome death!

Thy sweetness hath betrayed Thee, Lord!
    Dear Spirit! it is Thou;
Deeper and deeper in my heart
    I feel Thee neſtling now.

Self-Examination.

Whence Thou haſt come I need not aſk;
   But, O moſt gentle Dove!
O wherefore haſt Thou lit on one
   That so repays thy love?

Ah! that Thou mighteſt ſtay with me,
   Or else that I might die
While heart and soul are ſtill subdued
   With thy sweet maſtery.

Thy home is with the humble, Lord!
   The ſimple are thy reſt;
Thy lodging is in childlike hearts;
   Thou makeſt there thy neſt.

Dear Comforter! Eternal Love!
   If Thou wilt ſtay with me,
Of lowly thoughts and ſimple ways
   I'll build a neſt for Thee.

My heart, sweet Dove! I'll lend to Thee
   To mourn with at thy will;
My tongue ſhall be thy lute to try
   On ſinners' souls thy ſkill.

Who made this beating heart of mine,
   But Thou my heavenly Gueſt?
Let no one have it then but Thee,
   And let it be thy neſt.
                             Faber.

DRYNESS IN PRAYER.

O FOR the happy days gone by,
   When love ran smooth and free,
Days when my Spirit so enjoy'd
   More than earth's liberty!

O for the times when on my heart
   Long prayer had never pall'd,
Times when the ready thought of God
   Would come when it was call'd!

Then when I knelt to meditate,
   Sweet thoughts came o'er my soul,
Countless and bright and beautiful,
   Beyond my own control.

O who hath lock'd those fountains up?
   Those vifions who hath ftay'd?
What sudden act hath thus transform'd
   My sunfhine into fhade?

This freezing heart, O Lord! this will
   Dry as the desert sand,
Good thoughts that will not come, bad thoughts
   That come without command,—

Self-Examination.

A faith that seems not faith, a hope
    That cares not for its aim,
A love that none the hotter grows
    At Jesu's blessed name,—

The weariness of prayer, the mist
    O'er conscience overspread,
The chill repugnance to frequent
    The Feast of Angels' Bread :—

If this drear change be thine, O Lord!
    If it be thy sweet will,
Spare not, but to the very brim
    The bitter chalice fill.

But if it hath been sin of mine,
    O show that sin to me,
Not to get back the sweetness lost,
    But to make peace with Thee.

One thing alone, dear Lord! I dread ;—
    To have a secret spot
That separates my soul from Thee,
    And yet to know it not.

O when the tide of graces set
    So full upon my heart,
I know, dear Lord! how faithlessly
    I did my little part.

I know how well my heart hath earn'd
  A chaftisement like this,
In trifling many a grace away
  In self-complacent bliss.

But if this weariness hath come
  A present from on high,
Teach me to find the hidden wealth
  That in its depths may lie.

So in this darkness I can learn
  To tremble and adore,
To sound my own vile nothingness,
  And thus to love Thee more,—

To love Thee, and yet not to think
  That I can love so much,—
To have Thee with me, Lord! all day,
  Yet not to feel thy touch.

If I have served Thee, Lord! for hire,
  Hire which thy beauty fhow'd,
Ah! I can serve Thee now for naught,
  And only as my God.

O bleffed be this darkness then,
  This deep in which I lie,
And bleffed be all things that teach
  God's great supremacy.

Faber.

DISTRACTIONS IN PRAYER.

AH! deareft Lord! I cannot pray,
My fancy is not free;
Unmannerly diftractions come,
And force my thoughts from Thee.

The world that looks so dull all day
Glows bright on me at prayer,
And plans that afk no thought but then
Wake up and meet me there.

All nature one full fountain seems
Of dreamy fight and sound,
Which, when I kneel, breaks up its deeps,
And makes a deluge round.

Old voices murmur in my ear,
New hopes ftart into life,
And paft and future gayly blend
In one bewitching ftrife.

My very flefh has reftless fits;
My changeful limbs conspire
With all these phantoms of the mind
My inner self to tire.

Self-Examination.

I cannot pray; yet, Lord! Thou know'ſt
The pain it is to me
To have my vainly-ſtruggling thoughts
Thus torn away from Thee.

Prayer was not meant for luxury,
Or selfiſh paſtime sweet;
It is the proſtrate creature's place
At his Creator's feet.

Had I, dear Lord! no pleasure found
But in the thought of Thee,
Prayer would have come unsought, and been
A truer liberty.

Yet Thou art oft moſt present, Lord!
In weak diſtracted prayer;
A ſinner out of heart with self
Moſt often finds Thee there.

And prayer that humbles, sets the soul
From all illuſions free,
And teaches it how utterly,
Dear Lord! it hangs on Thee.

The soul, that on self-sacrifice
Is dutifully bent,
Will bless thy chaſtening hand that makes
Its prayer its puniſhment.

Ah, Jesus! why fhould I complain?
And why fear aught but fin?
Diftractions are but outward things;
Thy peace dwells far within!

These surface-troubles come and go,
Like rufflings of the sea;
The deeper depth is out of reach
To all, my God, but Thee!

Faber.

PREPARATIVE TO PRAYER.

WHEN thou doft talk with God—by prayer I mean—
Lift up pure hands, lay down all luft's defires;
Fix thoughts on heaven, present a conscience clean :
Since holy blame to mercy's throne aspires,
Confess faults' guilt, crave pardon for thy fin,
Tread holy paths, call grace to guide therein.

It is the spirit with reverence must obey
Our Maker's will, to practise what He taught :
Make not the flefh thy council when thou pray ;
'Tis enemy to every virtuous thought ;
It is the foe we daily feed and clothe ;
It is the prison that the soul doth loathe.

Even as Elias, mounting to the fky,
  Did caft his mantle to the earth behind;
So, when the heart presents the prayer on high,
  Exclude the world from traffic with the mind:
Lips near to God, and ranging heart within,
Is but vain babbling, and converts to fin.

As Abraham, ascending up the hill
  To sacrifice; his servants left below,
That he might act the great Commander's will,
  Without impeach to his obedient blow;
Even so the soul, remote from earthly things,
Should mount salvation's fhelter—mercy's wings.
Southwell.

CHRIST.

PASTOR ANIMARUM.

(From the Spanish.)

COME, wandering sheep, O come!
 I'll bind thee to my breast;
I'll bear thee to thy home,
 And lay thee down to rest.

I saw thee stray forlorn,
 And heard thee faintly cry,
And on the tree of scorn
 For thee I deign'd to die—
What greater proof could I
Give,—than to seek the tomb?
Come, wandering sheep, O come!

I shield thee from alarms,
 And wilt thou not be blest?
I bear thee in my arms;
 Thou, bear me in thy breast!
 O, this is love—come, rest—
This is a blissful doom.
Come, wandering sheep, O come!

DOMUS AUREA.

LIGHT! Light! Infinite Light!
  The mountains melted away:
Ten thousand thousand seraphim bright
  Were loft in a blaze of day:
For God was there, and beneath his feet
  A pavement of sapphires glow'd,*
As the mirror of glory transcendantly meet
  To reflect his own abode!

Love! Love! Infinite Love!
  The lowly Lady of grace
Bows underneath the o'erfhadowing Dove,
  Her eternal Son to embrace!
For God is there, the Ancient of Days,
  An Infant of human years:
Whilft angels around them inceffantly gaze,
  And nature is wrapt in tears!

Peace! Peace! Infinite Peace!
  A Golden House hath it found,
Whose ineffable beauty muft ever increase
  With immortality crown'd!
For God was there, the Lord of the skies,
  Whose loud alleluias ran,
From heaven to earth,—as Emmanuel lies
  In the arms of Mary for man!

Brydges.

* Exodus xxiv. 10.

Jesu dulcis memoria.

JESU! the very thought of Thee
    With sweetness fills my breaſt;
But sweeter far thy face to see,
    And in thy presence reſt.

Nor voice can sing, nor heart can frame,
    Nor can the memory find,
A sweeter sound than thy bleſt name,
    O Saviour of mankind!

O hope of every contrite heart,
    O joy of all the meek,
To those who fall, how kind Thou art!
    How good to those who seek!

But what to those who find? ah! this
    Nor tongue nor pen can show:
The love of Jesus, what it is,
    None but his loved ones know.

Jesus! our only joy be Thou,
    As Thou our prize wilt be;
Jesus! be Thou our glory now,
    And through eternity.

                    Breviary.

Christ.

Jesu Rex admirabilis.

O JESUS! King moſt wonderful!
Thou Conqueror renown'd!
Thou Sweetness moſt ineffable!
In whom all joys are found!

When once Thou viſiteſt the heart,
 Then truth begins to ſhine;
Then earthly vanities depart;
 Then kindles love divine.

O Jesu! Light of all below!
 Thou Fount of life and fire!
Surpaſſing all the joys we know,
 All that we can deſire:

May every heart confess thy name,
 And ever Thee adore;
And seeking Thee, itself inflame
 To seek Thee more and more.

Thee may our tongues forever bless;
 Thee may we love alone;
And ever in our lives express
 The image of thine own.

Breviary.

Jesu decus angelicum.

O JESU! Thou the beauty art
   Of angel worlds above;
Thy name is mufic to the heart,
   Enchanting it with love.

Celeftial sweetness unalloy'd!
   Who eat Thee hunger ftill;
Who drink of Thee ftill feel a void,
   Which naught but Thou can fill.

O my sweet Jesu! hear the fighs
   Which unto Thee I send;
To Thee mine inmoft spirit cries,
   My being's hope and end!

Stay with us, Lord, and with thy light
   Illume the soul's abyss;
Scatter the darkness of our night,
   And fill the world with bliss.

O Jesu! spotless Virgin flower!
   Our life and joy! to Thee
Be praise, beatitude, and power,
   Through all eternity.

Breviary.

Marentes oculi spargite lachrymas.

NOW let us sit and weep,
And fill our hearts with woe:
Pondering the shame, and torments deep,
Which Chrift from wicked men did undergo.

See! how the multitude,
With swords and ftaves, draw nigh:
See! how they smite, with buffets rude,
That head divine of awful majefty:

How, bound with cruel cord,
Chrift to the scourge is given;
And ruffians lift their hands, unawed,
Againft the King of Kings and Lord of Heaven.

Then roughly dragg'd to death,
Chrift on the Cross is flain;
And, as He dies, with parting breath,
Into his Father's hands gives back his soul again.

To Him who so much bore,
To gain for finners grace,
Be praise and glory evermore,
From the whole universal human race.

Breviary.

Quicunque certum quæritis.

ALL ye who seek a certain cure
   In trouble and diſtress,
Whatever sorrow vex the mind,
   Or guilt the soul oppress:

Jesus, who gave Himself for you
   Upon the Cross to die,
Opens to you his sacred Heart,—
   Oh, to that Heart draw nigh!

Ye hear how kindly He invites;
   Ye hear his words so bleſt;—
"All ye that labor, come to Me,
   And I will give you reſt."

What meeker than the Saviour's Heart?—
   As on the Cross He lay,
It did his murderers forgive,
   And for their pardon pray.

O Heart! thou joy of Saints on high!
   Thou Hope of ſinners here!
Attracted by those loving words,
   To Thee I lift my prayer.

Wash Thou my wounds in that dear Blood
Which forth from Thee doth flow;
New grace, new hope inspire; a new
And better heart bestow.
Breviary.

Summi Parentis filio.

TO Christ, the Prince of Peace,
And Son of God most high,
The Father of the world to come,—
Sing we with holy joy.

Deep in his Heart for us
The wound of love He bore;—
That love, which still He kindles in
The hearts that Him adore.

O Fount of endless life!
O Spring of waters clear!
O Flame celestial, cleansing all
Who unto Thee draw near!

Hide me in thy dear Heart,
For thither do I fly;
There seek thy grace through life, in death
Thine immortality.
Breviary.

JESUS CRUCIFIED.

O COME and mourn with me awhile;
  See, Mary calls us to her fide;
O come and let us mourn with her,—
  Jesus, our Love, is crucified!

Have we no tears to fhed for Him,
  While soldiers scoff and Jews deride?
Ah! look how patiently he hangs,—
  Jesus, our Love, is crucified!

His Mother cannot reach his face!
  She ftands in helpleffness befide,
Her heart is martyr'd with her Son's,—
  Jesus, our Love, is crucified!

Seven times He spoke, seven words of love,
  And all three hours his filence cried
For mercy on the souls of men:—
  Jesus, our Love, is crucified!

What was thy crime, my deareft Lord?
  By earth, by heaven, Thou haft been tried,
And guilty found of too much love;—
  Jesus, our Love, is crucified!

Found guilty of excess of love,
  It was thine own sweet will that tied
Thee tighter far than helpless nails ;—
  Jesus, our Love, is crucified !

Death came, and Jesus meekly bow'd ;
  His failing eyes He ſtrove to guide
With mindful love to Mary's face ;—
  Jesus, our Love, is crucified !

O break, O break, hard heart of mine !
  Thy weak self-love and guilty pride
His Pilate and his Judas were ;—
  Jesus, our Love, is crucified !

Come, take thy ſtand beneath the Cross,
  And let the blood from out that side
Fall gently on thee drop by drop ;—
  Jesus, our Love, is crucified !

A broken heart, a fount of tears,—
  Aſk, and they will not be denied ;
A broken heart love's cradle is ;—
  Jesus, our Love, is crucified !

O love of God ! O sin of Man !
  In this dread act your ſtrength is tried ;
And victory remains with love,
  For He, our Love, is crucified !

EASTER.

Ad regias agni dapes.

NOW at the Lamb's high royal feaſt
   In robes of saintly white we ſing,
Through the Red Sea in safety brought
   By Jesus our immortal King.

O depth of love! for us He drinks
   The chalice of his agony:
For us a victim on the Cross
   He meekly lays Him down to die.

And as the avenging Angel pass'd
   Of old the blood-besprinkled door;
As the cleft sea a paſſage gave,
   Then closed to whelm th' Egyptians o'er:

So Chriſt, our Paschal Sacrifice,
   Has brought us safe all perils through;
While for unleaven'd bread we need
   But heart ſincere and purpose true.

Hail, pureſt victim Heaven could find,
   The powers of Hell to overthrow!
Who didſt the chains of Death deſtroy;
   Who doſt the prize of Life beſtow.

Christ.

Hail, victor Chrift! hail, risen King!
To Thee alone belongs the crown;
Who haft the heavenly gates unbarr'd,
And dragg'd the Prince of darkness down.

O Jesus! from the death of fin
Keep us we pray; so fhalt Thou be
The everlafting Paschal joy
Of all the souls new-born in Thee.
Breviary.

LIGHT of the Soul, O Saviour bleft!
Soon as thy presence fills the breaft,
Darkness and guilt are put to flight,
And all is sweetness and delight.

Son of the Father! Lord moft high!
How glad is he who feels Thee nigh!
How sweet in Heaven thy beam doth glow,
Denied to eye of flefh below!

O Light of Light celeftial!
O Charity ineffable!
Come in thy hidden majefty;
Fill us with love, fill us with Thee.
Breviary.

Dies iræ dies illa.

NIGHER still, and still more nigh
 Draws the Day of Prophecy,
Doom'd to melt the earth and sky.

Oh, what trembling there shall be,
When the world its Judge shall see,
Coming in dread majesty!

Hark! the trump, with thrilling tone,
From sepulchral regions lone,
Summons all before the throne:

Time and Death it doth appall,
To see the buried ages all
Rise to answer at the call.

Now the books are open spread;
Now the writing must be read,
Which condemns the quick and dead:

Now, before the Judge severe
Hidden things must all appear;
Naught can pass unpunish'd here.

What shall guilty I then plead?
Who for me will intercede,
When the Saints shall comfort need?

King of dreadful Majesty!
Who dost freely justify!
Fount of Pity, save Thou me!

Recollect, O Love divine!
'Twas for this lost sheep of thine
Thou thy glory didst resign:

Satest wearied seeking me;
Sufferedst upon the tree:
Let not vain thy labor be.

Judge of Justice, hear my prayer!
Spare me, Lord, in mercy spare!
Ere the Reckoning-day appear.

Lo! thy gracious face I seek;
Shame and grief are on my cheek;
Sighs and tears my sorrow speak.

Thou didst Mary's guilt forgive;
Didst the dying thief receive;
Hence doth hope within me live.

Suppliant in the duſt I lie;
My heart a cinder, cruſh'd and dry;
Help me, Lord, when death is nigh!

Full of tears, and full of dread,
Is the day that wakes the dead,
Calling all, with solemn blaſt,
From the aſhes of the paſt.

Lord of mercy! Jesu bleſt!
Grant the Faithful light and reſt.
Missal.

Salutis humanæ Sator.

O THOU pure light of souls that love,
True joy of every human breaſt,
Sower of life's immortal seed,
Our Saviour and Redeemer bleſt!

Be Thou our guide, be Thou our goal;
Be Thou our pathway to the ſkies;
Our joy, when sorrow fills the soul;
In death our everlaſting prize.
Breviary.

ROCK OF AGES.

ROCK of Ages, cleft for me,
Let me hide myself in Thee;
Let the water and the blood,
From thy wounded side which flowed,
Be of sin the double cure;
Save from wrath and make me pure.

In my hand no price I bring,
Simply to thy Cross I cling;
Naked come to Thee for dress,
Helpless look to Thee for grace,
Foul, I to the Fountain fly;
Wash me, Saviour, or I die.

While I draw this fleeting breath,
When my eyes shall close in death,
When I rise to worlds unknown,
And behold Thee on thy throne;
Rock of Ages, cleft for me,
Let me hide myself in Thee.

Toplady.

THE DAY OF JUDGMENT.

Dies iræ, dies illa.

L O! He comes with clouds descending,
    Once for favor'd finners flain:
Thousand—thousand saints attending,
    Swell the triumph of his train:
    Alleluia! Alleluia!
    Jesus Chrift fhall ever reign!

See the universe in motion,
    Sinking on her funeral pyre,—
Earth diffolving, and the ocean
    Vanifhing in final fire:—
    Hark, the trumpet! Hark, the trumpet!
    Loud proclaims that Day of Ire!

Graves have yawn'd in countless numbers,—
    From the duft the dead arise:
Millions, out of filent flumbers,
    Wake in overwhelm'd surprise;
    Where creation,—Where creation,
    Wreck'd and torn in ruin lies!

See the Judge our nature wearing,
    Pure, ineffable, divine:—
See the great Archangel bearing

High in heaven the myftic fign:
Cross of Glory! Cross of Glory!
Chrift be in that moment mine!

See Redemption,* long expected,
　In tranfcendant pomp appear,—
All his saints by man rejected,
　Throng in gathering legions near:
Melt, ye mountains! Melt, ye mountains!
　Into smoke,—for God is here!

Every eye fhall then behold Him
　Robed in awful majefty:—
Those that set at naught, and sold Him,
　Pierced and nail'd Him to a tree,—
Deeply wailing,—Deeply wailing,
　Shall the true Meffiah see!

Lo! the laft long separation!
　As the cleaving crowds divide;
And one dread adjudication
　Sends each soul to either fide!
Lord of mercy! Lord of mercy!
　How fhall I that day abide!

Oh! may thine own Bride and Spirit
　Then avert a dreadful doom,—
And me summon to inherit
　An eternal blissful home:—

* Romans viii. 23.

Ah! come quickly! Ah! come quickly!
Let thy second Advent come!

Yea, Amen! Let all adore Thee,
  On thine amaranthine throne!
Saviour,—take the power and glory,
  Claim the kingdom for thine own!
Men and angels: Men and angels,
  Kneel and bow to Thee alone!
                    Brydges.

Tinctam ergo Christi sanguine.

OH, turn those bleſſed points, all bathed
    In Jesu's blood, on me;
Mine were the ſins that wrought his death,
    Mine be the penalty.

Pierce through my feet, my hands, my heart;
    So may some drop diſtill
Of blood divine, into my soul,
    And all its evils heal.

So ſhall my feet be ſlow to ſin,
    Harmless my hands ſhall be;
So from my wounded heart ſhall each
    Forbidden paſſion flee.
                    Breviary.

MOST HOLY NAME OF JESUS.

OH! that it were as it was wont to be,
When thy old friends of fire, all full of Thee,
Fought againſt frowns with smiles! gave glorious chase
To persecutions, and againſt the face
Of death and fierceſt dangers durſt, with brave
And sober pace march on to meet a grave.
On their bold breaſts about the world they bore Thee.
And to the teeth of hell ſtood up to teach Thee;
In centre of their inmoſt souls they wore Thee,
Where racks and torments ſtrived in vain to reach Thee.
Each wound of theirs was thy new morning,
And reënthroned Thee in thy rosy neſt.
With bluſh of thine own blood thy day adorning:
It was the wit of love o'erflowed the bounds
Of wrath, and made the way through all these wounds.
Welcome, dear, all-adored name!
For sure there is no knee
That knows not Thee;
  Or, if there be such sons of ſhame,
Alas! what will they do,
  When ſtubborn rocks ſhall bow,
And hills hang down their heaven-saluting heads,
  To seek for humble beds
Of duſt, where, in the baſhful ſhades of night,
Next to their own low nothing they may lie,

And crouch before the dazzling light of thy dread majesty?
They that by love's mild dictate now
    Will not adore Thee,
Shall then with just confusion bow,
    And break before Thee.
Crashaw.

RISE—GLORIOUS CONQUEROR, RISE.

RISE—glorious Conqueror, rise;
    Into thy native skies,—
        Assume thy right:
And where in many a fold
The clouds are backward roll'd—
Pass through those gates of gold,
        And reign in light!

Victor o'er death and hell!
Cherubic legions swell
        The radiant train:
Praises all heaven inspire;
Each angel sweeps his lyre,
And waves his wings of fire,—
        Thou Lamb once slain!

Enter, Incarnate God!—
No feet, but thine, have trod
        The serpent down:

Blow the full trumpets, blow!
Wider yon portals throw!
Saviour—triumphant—go,
    And take thy crown!

Lion of Judah—Hail!—
And let thy name prevail
    From age to age:
Lord of the rolling years,—
Claim for thine own the spheres,
For Thou hast bought with tears
    Thy heritage!

Yet—who are these behind,
In numbers more than mind
    Can count or say—
Clothed in immortal stoles,
Illumining the poles—
A galaxy of souls,
    In white array?

And then was heard afar
Star answering to star—
    Lo! these have come,
Followers of Him, who gave
His life, their lives to save;
And now their palms they wave,
    Brought safely home.

Brydges.

HEAD of the Hofts in glory!
We joyfully adore Thee,—
    Thy church on earth below,
Blending with those on high,—
Where through the azure sky
Thy saints in ecftasy,—
    For ever glow!

Then raise the song of gladness,
To diffipate our sadness—
    Along this vale of tears:
We wend our weary way
Up towards the realms of day,—
And watch,—and wait,—and pray,
    Conftant in fears!

Holy Apoftles! beaming
With radiance brightly ftreaming
    From diadems of power;
Call on the awful name,—
That we, through flood and flame
The gospel may proclaim
    In every hour!

Martyrs!—whose myftic legions
March o'er yon heavenly regions
    In triumph round and round;

Christ.

Wave—wave your banners—wave!
For Christ—our Saviour, clave
For Death itself a grave,—
  In hell profound!

Saints!—in fair circles, cafting
Rich trophies everlafting
  At Jesu's pierced feet,—
Amidst our rude alarms,
Stretch forth your conquering arms,
That we too, safe from harms,
  In heaven may meet!

Virgins!—in bliss transcendent,
Whose coronals resplendent
  Unwithering bloom:
Exalt, in ceaseless lays,
Him whom all anthems praise,
And oft our spirits raise
  With your perfume!

Angels—Archangels! glorious
Guards of the church victorious!
  Sing to the Lamb!
Crown Him with crowns of light,—
One of the Three by right,—
Love,—Majesty,—and Might,—
  The 'Great I AM!

Brydges.

"AND JESUS WEPT."

St. John xi. 35.

BRIGHT were the mornings first impearl'd
  O'er earth, and sea, and air;
The birthdays of a rifing world—
  For power divine was there.

But fairer shone the tears of Christ
  For Lazarus, o'er his grave;
Since love divine bedew'd the sod
  Of one He sought to save.

Sweet drops of grace, the pledges given
  Of Mercy's mighty plan,—
That He, who was the Prince of heaven,
  Had pity upon man!

Let us thy dear example, Lord,
  Fix'd in our memories keep,—
That we, obedient to thy word,
  May weep with those that weep.

Brydges.

BRIGHT cherubim and seraphim,
In one myfterious crowd,
Expand the everlafting hymn
That rolls from cloud to cloud.

Odors, in folds of fragrant fumes,
Pervade the ravifh'd fkies;
Whilst angels form, with arching plumes,
A firmament of eyes!*

They gaze, and as they gaze, they shine,
And as they shine, admire,
With adoration all divine,—
All love,—all life,—all fire!

No temple there is made with hands
By human priefthood trod;
Alone the once-slain Victim stands,
The living Lamb of God!

Brydges.

* Ezek. i. 18–23: x. 12. Apocal. iv. 8.

Quicunque Christum quæritis.

ALL ye who seek, in hope and love,
For your dear Lord, look up above!
Where, traced upon the azure fky,
Faith may a glorious form descry.

Lo! on the trembling verge of light
A something all divinely bright!
Immortal, infinite, sublime!
Older than chaos, space, or time!

Hail, Thou, the Gentiles' mighty Lord!
All hail, O Israel's King adored!
To Abraham sworn in ages paft,
And to his seed while earth shall laft.

To Thee the prophets witness bear;
Of Thee the Father doth declare,
That all who would his glory see,
Muft hear and muft believe in Thee.
Breviary.

SAINTS, MARTYRS, &c.

ST. JOHN THE BAPTIST.

Antra deserti teneris sub annis.

IN caves of the lone wilderness thy youth
    Thou hiddeft, fhunning the rude throng of men,
And guarding the pure treasure of thy soul
      From the leaft touch of fin.

There to thy sacred limbs the camel gave
A garment coarse; the rock a bed supplied;
The ftream thy thirft; locufts and honey wild
      Thy hunger satisfied.

Oh, bleft beyond the Prophets of old time!
They of the Saviour sang that was to be:
Him present to announce, and show to all,
      Was granted but to thee.

Through the wide earth was never mortal man
Born holier than John; to whom was given
The guilty world's Baptizer to baptize,
      And ope the door of Heaven.
                        Breviary.

CHRIST.

Christe, sanctorum decus angelorum.

O CHRIST! the beauty of the angel worlds!
Of man the Saviour and Redeemer bleſt!
Grant us one day to mount the path of light,
    And in thy glory reſt.

Angel of Peace! thou, Michael, from above,
Come down, amid the homes of man to dwell;
And banish wars, with all their tears and blood,
    Back to their native Hell.

Angel of Strength! thou, Gabriel, caſt out
Thine ancient foes, usurpers of thy reign;
The temples of thy triumph round the globe
    Reviſit once again.

And Raphael, Physician of the soul,—
Let him descend from his pure halls of light,
To heal the ſick, and guide each doubtful course
    Through all our life aright.

Thou too, O Virgin, with the angel choirs,
Mother of Light, and Queen of Peace! descend
And bring with thee the radiant Court of Heaven
    Thy children to befriend.

Breviary.

OF MANY MARTYRS.

Sanctorum meritis inclyta gaudia.

SING we the peerless deeds of martyr'd Saints,
 Their glorious merits, and their portion bleſt;
Of all the conquerors the world has seen,
 The greateſt and the beſt.

Them in their day th' insensate world abhorr'd,
Because they did forsake it, Lord, for Thee;
Finding it all a barren waſte, devoid
 Of fruit, or flower, or tree.

They trod beneath them every threat of man,
And came victorious all torments through;
The iron hooks, which piecemeal tore their flesh,
 Could not their souls subdue.

Scourged, crucified, like ſheep to ſlaughter led,
Unmurmuring they met their cruel fate;
For conscious innocence their souls upheld,
 In patient virtue great.

What tongue those joys, O Jesus, can disclose,
Which for thy martyr'd Saints Thou doſt prepare!
Happy who in thy pains, thrice happy those
 Who in thy glory ſhare!

Our faults, our sins, our miseries remove,
Great Deity supreme, immortal King!
Grant us thy peace, grant us thine endless love
　Through endless years to sing.
　　　　　　　　　　　Breviary.

　　　　Æterna Christi munera.

THE Lord's eternal gifts,
　　Th' Apostles' mighty praise,
Their victories, and high reward,
　Sing we in joyful lays.

　Lords of the churches they;
　Triumphant Chiefs of war;
Brave Soldiers of the Heavenly Court;
　True lights for evermore.

　Theirs was the Saints' high Faith;
　And quenchless Hope's pure glow;
And perfect Charity, which laid
　The world's fell tyrant low.

　In them the Father shone;
　In them the Son o'ercame;
In them the Holy Spirit wrought,
　And fill'd their hearts with flame.
　　　　　　　　　　　Breviary.

ST. STEPHEN.

O qui tuo dux Martyrum.

O CAPTAIN of the Martyr Hoſt!
  O peerless in renown!
Not from the fading flowers of earth
  Weave we for thee a crown.

The ſtones that smote thee, in thy blood
  Made glorious and divine,
All in a halo heavenly bright
  About thy temples ſhine.

The scars upon thy sacred brow
  Throw beams of glory round;
The splendors of thy bruised face
  The very sun confound.

Oh, earlieſt Victim sacrificed
  To thy dear Victim Lord!
Oh, earlieſt witness to the Faith
  Of thy Incarnate God!

Thou to the heavenly Canaan firſt
  Through the Red Sea didſt go,
And to the Martyrs' countless Hoſt,
  Their path of glory ſhow.

Erewhile a servant of the poor,—
Now at the Lamb's high Feaſt,
In blood-empurpled robe array'd,
A welcome nuptial gueſt !

Breviary.

ST. JOHN THE BAPTIST.

O nimis felix meritique celsi.

O BLESSED Saint, of snow-white purity!
   Dweller in waſtes forlorn !
O mightieſt of the Martyr hoſt on high !
   Greateſt of Prophets born !

Of all the diadems that on the brows
   Of Saints in glory ſhine,
Not one with brighter, purer halo glows,
   In Heaven's high Court, than thine.

Oh ! upon us thy tender, pitying gaze
   Caſt down from thy dread throne ;
Straighten our crooked, smooth our rugged ways,
   And break our hearts of ſtone.

So may the world's Redeemer find us meet
   To offer Him a place,
Where He may set his ever-bleſſed feet
   Coming with gifts of grace.

Breviary.

ST. FRANCIS XAVIER.

LO! on the flope of yonder fhore
  Beneath that lonely fhed,—
A saint hath found his conflicts o'er,
  And laid his dying head!

No gloom of fear hath glazed his eye,
  For though loud billows roll,—
The Aurora of Eternity
  Is rifing on his soul.

The glorious Saviour of his love
  Receives him in his arms,
And bears him, like a ransom'd dove,
  Away from all alarms!

Champion of Jesus!—man of God,
  Servant of Chrift, well done!
Thy path of thorns hath now been trod,
  Thy red-cross crown is won!

O'er the wide wafte of watery waves,
  And leagues on leagues of land,
Amidft a wilderness of graves,
  With death on every hand,—

He flew to woo and win a world;
  That men might kiss the feet
Of Him, whose banner he unfurl'd,—
  Father,—Son,—Paraclete!

His tongue, the Spirit's two-edged sword,
  Had magic in its blade,—
For while it smote with every word,
  It heal'd the wounds it made!

His lips were love, his touch was power,
  His thoughts were vivid flame,
The flashes of a thunder-shower—
  Where'er, or when they came!

Around him shone the light of life,
  Before him darkness fell—
Satan receded from the strife,
  And sought his native hell!

Yet, who so humbly walk'd as he,
  A conqueror in the field,
Wreathing the rose of victory
  Around his radiant shield?

As silvery clouds, at eventide,
  Float on the balmy gale,
Nor seem to heed the stars they hide
  Behind their fleecy veil;

So lowly sense of flighteft worth
 Frefh graces o'er him threw;
For he unconscious lived on earth,
 Of all the praise he drew!

Champion of Jesus! on that breaft
 From whence thy fervor flow'd,
Thou haft obtain'd eternal reft,
 The bosom of thy God!
Brydges.

ST. ELIZABETH, QUEEN OF PORTUGAL.

Domare cordis impetus Elizabeth.

PURE, meek, with soul serene,
 Sweeter to her it was to serve unseen
Her God, than reign a queen.

Now far above our fight,
Enthroned upon the azure ftar-paved height,
 She reigns in realms of light;

So long as time fhall flow,
Teaching to all who sit on thrones below,
 The good that power can do.
Breviary.

MARTYRDOM OF ST. LUCY.

WE watch'd, as she linger'd all the day
    Beneath the torturer's fkill;
And we pray'd that the spirit might pass away,
    And the weary frame be ftill.
'Twas a long fharp ftruggle from darkness to light,
    And the pain was fierce and sore;
But she, we knew, in her lateft fight
    Muft be more than conqueror!

Oh, what a change had the prison wrought
    Since we gazed upon her laft!
And mournful the leffons her thin frame taught
    Of the sufferings she had paft:
Of pain and fickness—not of fear!
    There was courage in her eye:
And she enter'd the amphitheatre
    As to triumph, and not to die!

And once, when we could not bear to see
    Her sufferings, and turn'd the head,
" His rod and His ftaff they comfort me,"
    The virgin martyr said:
It was near the setting of the sun,
    And her voice wax'd faint and low;
And we knew that her race was well-nigh run,
    And her time drew near to go.

We could almoſt deem the clouds that roll'd
    In the ruddy sun's decline
To be chariots of fire and horses of gold
    On the ſteep of Mount Aventine :
Yea, guardian angels bent their way
    From their own ſkies' cloudless blue,
And a triumph more glorious was thine to-day
    Than ever the Cæsar knew!

We lay thee here in the narrow cell
    Where thy friends and brethren ſleep;
And we carve the palm, of thy lot to tell,
    And we do not dare to weep.
Hopefully wait we God's holy time
    That ſhall call us to ſhare thy reſt;
Till then, we muſt dwell in an alien clime,
    While thou art in Abraham's breaſt.

Neale.

THE SISTER OF CHARITY.

SHE once was a lady of honor and wealth;
Bright glow'd in her features the roses of health;
Her vesture was blended of silk and of gold,
And her motion shook perfume from every fold:
Joy revell'd around her—love shone at her side,
And gay was her smile as the glance of a bride;
And light was her step in the mirth-sounding hall,
When she heard of the daughters of Vincent de Paul.

She felt in her spirit the summons of grace,
That call'd her to live for her suffering race;
And, heedless of pleasure, of comfort, of home,
Rose quickly, like Mary, and answer'd "I come."
She put from her person the trappings of pride,
And pass'd from her home with the joy of a bride,
Nor wept at the threshold as onward she moved—
For her heart was on fire in the cause it approved.

Lost ever to fashion—to vanity lost,
That beauty that once was the song and the toast—
No more in the ball-room that figure we meet,
But gliding at dusk to the wretch's retreat.
Forgot in the halls is that high-sounding name,
For the Sister of Charity blushes at fame:

Forgot are the claims of her riches and birth,
For she barters for heaven the glory of earth.

Those feet, that to music could gracefully move,
Now bear her alone on the miffion of love;
Those hands, that once dangled the perfume and gem,
Are tending the helpless, or lifted for them;
That voice, that once echo'd the song of the vain,
Now whispers relief to the bosom of pain;
And the hair that was shining with diamond and pearl,
Is wet with the tears of the penitent girl.

Her down-bed, a pallet—her trinkets, a bead,
Her lustre—one taper, that serves her to read;
Her sculpture—the crucifix nail'd by her bed;
Her paintings,—one print of the thorn-crowned head;
Her cushion—the pavement that wearies her knees;
Her music—the psalm, or the sigh of disease:
The delicate lady lives mortified there,
And the feast is forsaken for fasting and prayer.

Yet not to the service of heart and of mind,
Are the cares of that heaven-minded virgin confined:
Like Him whom she loves, to the mansions of grief
She hastes with the tidings of joy and relief.
She strengthens the weary—she comforts the weak,
And soft is her voice in the ear of the sick;
Where want and affliction on mortals attend,
The Sister of Charity *there* is a friend.

Unshrinking where pestilence scatters his breath,
Like an angel she moves, mid the vapors of death;
Where rings the loud musket, and flashes the sword,
Unfearing she walks, for she follows her Lord.
How sweetly she bends o'er each plague-tainted face,
With looks that are lighted with holiest grace;
How kindly she dresses each suffering limb,
For she sees in the wounded the image of Him.

Behold her, ye worldly! behold her, ye vain!
Who shrink from the pathway of virtue and pain;
Who yield up to pleasure your nights and your days,
Forgetful of service, forgetful of praise.
Ye lazy philosophers, self-seeking men—
Ye fireside philanthropists, great at the pen,
How stands in the balance your eloquence weigh'd
With the life and the deeds of that high-born maid?
Griffin.

MARTYRDOM OF THE INNOCENTS.

LOVELY flowers of martyrs, hail!
　Smitten by the tyrant foe
On life's threſhold,—as the gale
　Strews the roses ere they blow.

Firſt to die for Chriſt, sweet lambs!
　At the very altar ye,
With your fatal crowns and palms,
　Sport in your ſimplicity.
Breviary.

IN MEMORIAM.

HOLY and innocent were all his ways;
　Sweet, temperate, unſtain'd;
His life was prayer,—his every breath was praise,
　While breath to him remain'd.

To God, of all the centre and the source,
　Be power and glory given;
Who sways the mighty world through all its course,
　From the bright throne of Heaven.
Breviary.

ST. MARY MAGDALENE.

Pater superni luminis.

FATHER of lights! one glance of Thine,
　　Whose eyes the Universe control,
Fills Magdalene with holy love,
　　And melts the ice within her soul.

Her precious ointment forth she brings,
　　Upon those sacred feet to pour;
She washes them with burning tears;
　　And with her hair she wipes them o'er.

Impassioned to the Cross she clings;
　　Nor fears beside the tomb to stay;
Of ruffian soldiers naught she recks,
　　For love has cast all fear away.

O Christ, thou very Love itself!
　　Blest hope of man, through Thee forgiven!
So touch our spirits from above,
　　And purify our souls for Heaven.

Breviary.

COMMUNION SERVICE.

LO! upon the Altar lies,
Hidden deep from human eyes,
Bread of Angels from the fkies,
Made the food of mortal man:
Children's meat to dogs denied;
In old types forefignified
In the manna Heaven-supplied,
Isaac, and the Paschal Lamb.

Jesus! Shepherd of the sheep!
Thou thy flock in safety keep.
Living Bread! thy life supply;
Strengthen us, or else we die;
Fill us with celeftial grace:
Thou who feedeft us below!
Source of all we have or know!
Grant that with thy Saints above,
Sitting at the feaft of love,
We may see Thee face to face.
Missal.

ASPIRATIONS AFTER COMMUNION.

PRESERVE, my Jesus, oh preserve
 My soul to everlasting life.
Oh, may this bleft communion serve
 To aid my soul in paffion's ftrife:
Oh, may thy body, may thy blood,
Be to my soul a saving food,
To fill it ftill with life and grace,
And every finful ftain efface!

To bless Thee be my sole employ,
 My God, my Saviour, great and kind!
Inflame my heart with holy joy;
 Teach me, in praifing Thee, to find
Warm thoughts and feelings warm, whose glow
My gratitude may aptly fhow.
But no, my God! nor word, nor thought,
Could bless and praise Thee as I ought.
Weak praise were mine. Do Thou inspire
My soul with love and living fire.
Oh, may this cold and lowly breaft
Be warm'd by Thee, its God, its gueft.
May it by Thee be moved to love,
And taught thy saving grace to improve.
Take, then, my thoughts from all but Thee.
 To Thee, may ev'ry impulse tend.

Communion Service.

What 'vails to tell my misery?
I have my God—my gueſt—my friend:
So be His praise my only theme!
All wants my Saviour will redeem.
My Saviour knows whate'er I need—
He gives Himself: and ſhall I plead
For other boons? No! let me raise
Mine ev'ry thought in love and praise.
Dear Lord, no other prayer I form
Than for devotion pure and warm.
May warm devotion fill my soul;
May love for Thee each thought control;
May piety increase; and prayer
Mine ev'ry thought, word, aċtion ſhare;
The gift of love my sole requeſt—
Thou, God of love! wilt grant the reſt.

Dear Lord! may this Communion prove
A never-failing bond of love.
Forgive my coldness, and supply
Mine every weak deficiency.
May thy beſt grace suffice for all,
And every wayward sense enthrall:
Such grace on every feeling pour
As ne'er may leave thy servant more:
Each hope, each impulse firmly bind
In grace to Thee, my Saviour kind:
Such saving grace, dear Lord, be given
As leads the happy soul to heaven.

J. R. Beste.

DEDICATION OF A CHURCH.

Alto ex Olympi vertice.

FROM higheſt Heaven, the Father's Son,
  Descending like that myſtic ſtone
Cut from a mountain without hands,
Came down below, and filled all lands;
Uniting, midway in the ſky,
His House on earth, and House on high.

That House on high,—it ever rings
With praises of the King of kings;
For ever there, on harps divine,
They hymn th' eternal One and Trine;
We, here below, the ſtrain prolong,
And faintly echo Sion's song.

O Lord of lords inviſible!
With thy pure light this temple fill:
Hither, oft as invoked, descend;
Here to thy people's prayer attend:
Here, through all hearts, for evermore,
The Spirit's quick'ning graces pour.

Here may the Faithful, day by day,
In kneeling adoration pray;
And here receive from thy dear love
The bleſſings of that home above;
Till, loosen'd from this mortal chain,
Its everlaſting joys they gain.
Breviary.

Cælestis urbs Jerusalem.

JERUSALEM, thou City bleſt!
Dear viſion of celeſtial reſt!
Which far above the ſtarry ſky,
Piled up with living ſtones on high,
Art, as a Bride, encircled bright,
With million angel forms of light:

Oh, wedded in a prosperous hour!
The Father's glory was thy dower;
The Spirit all His graces ſhed,
Thou peerless Queen, upon thy head;
When Chriſt espoused thee for his Bride,
O City bright and glorified!

Thy gates a pearly luſtre pour;
Thy gates are open evermore;

And thither evermore draw nigh
All who for Chriſt have dared to die;
Or smit with love of their dear Lord,
Have pains endured, and joys abhorr'd.

Thou too, O Church, which here we see!
No easy taſk hath builded thee.
Long did the chisels ring around!
Long did the mallets' blows rebound!
Long work'd the head and toil'd the hand!
Ere ſtood thy ſtones as now they ſtand!

Breviary.

MISCELLANEOUS.

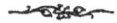

THE ASCENSION.

WHY is thy face so lit with smiles,
   Mother of Jesus! why?
And wherefore is thy beaming look
   So fixed upon the fky?

From out thine overflowing eyes
   Bright lights of gladness part,
As though some gufhing fount of joy
   Had broken in thy heart.

Mother! how canft thou smile to-day?
   How can thine eyes be bright,
When He, thy Life, thy Love, thine All,
   Hath vanifh'd from thy fight?

His rifing form on Olivet
   A summer's fhadow caft;
The branches of the hoary trees
   Droop'd as the fhadow paff'd.

And as He rose with all his train
  Of righteous souls around,
His bleſſing fell into thine heart,
  Like dew into the ground.

Down ſtoop'd a ſilver cloud from heaven,
  The Eternal Spirit's car,
And on the leſſening viſion went,
  Like some receding ſtar.

The silver cloud hath sail'd away,
  The ſkies are blue and free;
The road that viſion took is now
  Sunſhine and vacancy.

The Feet which thou haſt kiſſ'd so oft,
  Those living Feet, are gone;
Mother! thou canſt but ſtoop and kiss
  Their print upon the ſtone.

Yes! He hath left thee, Mother dear!
  His throne is far above;
How canſt thou be so full of joy
  When thou haſt loſt thy Love?

O surely earth's poor sunſhine now
  To thee mere gloom appears,
When He is gone who was its light
  For Three-and-Thirty Years.

Why do not thy sweet hands detain
   His Feet upon their way?
O why doth not the Mother speak
   And bid her Son to ſtay?

Ah no! thy love is rightful love,
   From all self-seeking free;
The change that is such gain to Him
   Can be no loss to thee!

'Tis sweet to feel our Saviour's love,
   To feel his presence near;
Yet loyal love his glory holds
   A thousand times more dear.

Who would have known the way to love
   Our Jesus as we ought,
If thou in varied joy and woe
   Hadſt not that leſſon taught?

Ah! never is our love so pure
   As when refined by pain,
Or when God's glory upon earth
   Finds in our loss its gain!

True love is worſhip: Mother dear!
   O gain for us the light
To love, because the creature's love
   Is the Creator's right!

Faber.

HYMN TO MY GUARDIAN ANGEL.

(For Children.)

Dear Angel! ever at my side,
  How loving muſt thou be
To leave thy home in Heaven to guard
  A little child like me.

Thy beautiful and ſhining face
  I see not, though so near;
The sweetness of thy soft low voice
  I am too deaf to hear.

I cannot feel thee touch my hand
  With preſſure light and mild,
To check me, as my mother did
  When I was but a child.

But I have felt thee in my thoughts
  Fighting with ſin for me;
And when my heart loves God, I know
  The sweetness is from thee.

And when, dear Spirit! I kneel down
  Morning and night to prayer,
Something there is within my heart
  Which tells me thou art there.

Yes! when I pray thou prayeſt too—
Thy prayer is all for me;
But when I sleep, thou sleepeſt not,
But watcheſt patiently.

Ah me! how lovely they muſt be
Whom God has glorified;
Yet one of them, O sweeteſt thought!
Is ever at my ſide.

And thou in life's laſt hour wilt bring
A freſh supply of grace,
And afterwards wilt let me kiss
Thy beautiful bright face.

Then for thy sake, dear Angel! now
More humble will I be:
But I am weak, and when I fall,
O weary not for me:

Then love me, love me, Angel dear!
And I will love thee more;
And help me when my soul is caſt
Upon the eternal ſhore.

Faber.

HYMN OF THE CALABRIAN SHEPHERDS.

DARKER and darker fall around
　　The ſhadows from the pine ;
It is the hour with hymn and prayer
　　To gather round thy ſhrine.

Hear us, sweet Mother! thou haſt known
　　Our earthly hopes and fears,
The bitterness of mortal toil
　　The tenderness of tears.

We pray thee firſt for absent ones,
　　Those who knelt with us here—
The father, brother, and the son,
　　The diſtant and the dear.

We pray thee for the little bark
　　Upon the ſtormy sea ;
Affection's anxiousness of love,
　　Is it not known to thee ?

The soldier, he who only sleeps
　　His head upon his brand,
Who only in a dream can see
　　His own beloved land.

The wandering Minstrel, he who gave
   Thy hymns his earliest tone,
Who strives to teach a foreign tongue
   The music of his own.

Kind Mother, let them see again
   Their own Italian shore;
Back to the home, which wanting them,
   Seems like a home no more.

Madonna, keep the cold north wind
   Amid his native seas,
So that no withering blight come down
   Upon our olive trees.

And bid the sunshine glad our hills,
   The dew rejoice our vines,
And bid the healthful sea-breeze sweep
   In music through the pines.

Pray for us that our hearts and homes
   Be kept in fear and love;
Love for all things around our path,
   And fear for those above.

Thy soft blue eyes are fill'd with tears,
   Oh! let them wash away
The soil of our unworthiness:—
   Pray for us, Mother, pray!

We know how vain the fleeting flowers
　Around thine altar hung;
We know how humble is the hymn
　Before thine image sung.

But wilt thou not accept the wreath,
　And sanctify the lay;
We truſt to thee our hopes and fears,—
　Pray for us, Mother, pray!

Stabat Mater dolorosa.

AT the Cross her ſtation keeping,
　　Stood the mournful Mother weeping,
　Close to Jesus to the laſt:
Through her heart, his sorrow ſharing,
All his bitter anguiſh bearing,
　Now at length the sword had paſſ'd.

Oh, how sad and sore diſtreſſ'd
Was that Mother highly bleſt
　Of the sole-begotten One!
Chriſt above in torment hangs;
She beneath beholds the pangs
　Of her dying glorious Son.

Is there one who would not weep,
Whelm'd in miseries so deep
　Chriſt's dear Mother to behold?
Can the human heart refrain
From partaking in her pain,
　In that Mother's pain untold?

Bruised, derided, cursed, defiled,
She beheld her tender Child
　All with bloody scourges rent;
For the ſins of his own nation,
Saw Him hang in desolation,
　Till his Spirit forth He sent.

O thou Mother! fount of love!
Touch my spirit from above.
　Make my heart with thine accord:
Make me feel as thou haſt felt;
Make my soul to glow and melt
　With the love of Chriſt my Lord.

Breviary.

PORTUGUESE HYMN.

STAR of the wide and pathless sea,
   Who loveſt on mariners to ſhine,
These votive garments wet, to thee
   We hang, within thy holy ſhrine.
When o'er us flaſh'd the surging brine,
Amid the warring waters toſſ'd,
   From earthly aid we turn'd to thine,
And hoped, when other hope was loſt.
     Ave Maris Stella!

Star of the vaſt and howling main,
   When dark and lone is all the ſky,
And mountain waves o'er ocean's plain,
   Erect their ſtormy heads on high;
When matrons by the hearthſtone ſigh,
They raise their weeping eyes to thee;
   The ſtar of ocean heeds their cry,
And saves the foundering bark at sea.
     Ave Maris Stella!

Star of the dark and ſtormy sea,
   When, wreaking tempeſts round us rave
Thy gentle virgin form we see,
   Bright riſing o'er the hoary wave.

The howling ſtorms that seem to crave
Their victims, ſink in muſic sweet;
The surging seas recede, to pave
The path beneath thy gliſtening feet.
  Ave Maris Stella!

Star of the desert waters wild,
 Who, pitying, hear'ſt the seaman's cry,
The Lord of Mercy, as a child,
 On that chaſte bosom loved to lie;
 While soft the chorus of the ſky
Their hymns of tender mercy ſing,
 And angel voices named on high
The Mother of the Heavenly King.
  Ave Maris Stella!

Star of the deep! at that bleſt name
 The waves ſleep ſilent round the keel,
The tempeſts wild their fury tame,
 That made the deep foundations reel;
 The soft celeſtial accents ſteal
So soothing through the realms of woe,
 That suffering souls a respite feel
From torture in the depths below.
  Ave Maris Stella!

Star of the mild and placid seas,
 Whom rainbow rays of mercy crown,
Whose name thy faithful Portuguese,
 O'er all that to the depths go down,

With hymns of grateful transport own ;
When gathering clouds obscure their light,
And heaven aſſumes an awful frown,
The ſtar of ocean glitters bright.
   Ave Maris Stella !

Star of the deep! when angel lyres
   To hymn thy holy name eſſay,
In vain a mortal harp aspires
   To mingle in the mighty lay !
Mother of Chriſt! one living ray
Of hope our grateful bosoms fires,
   When ſtorms and tempeſts pass away,
To join the bright immortal choirs.
   Ave Maris Stella !

THE MISSION OF THE HOLY GHOST.

NO track is on the sunny ſky,
   No footprints on the air ;
Jesus hath gone ; the face of earth
   Is desolate and bare.

The bleſſed feet of Mary's Son,
   They tread the ſtreets no more ;
His soul-converting voice gives not
   Its muſic as before.

His Mother fits all worshipful
  With her majestic mien;
The princes of the infant Church
  Are gather'd round their Queen.

They gaze on her with raptured eyes,
  Her features are like his,
Her presence is their ample strength,
  Her face reflects their bliss.

That Upper Room is heaven on earth;
  Within its precincts lie
All that earth has of faith, or hope,
  Or heaven-born charity.

The Eye of God looks down on them,
  His love is centred there;
His Spirit yearns to be o'ercome
  By their sweet strife of prayer.

The Mother prays her mighty prayer,
  In accents meek and faint,
And highest heaven is quick to own
  The beautiful constraint.

The Eternal Son takes up the prayer
  Upon his royal throne;
The Son his human Mother hears,
  The Sire his holy Son.
              Faber.

THOU ART OF ALL CREATED THINGS.

THOU art of all created things,
O Lord, the effence and the cause—
The source and centre of all bliss;
What are those veils of woven light,
Where sun and moon and ftars unite—
The purple morn, the spangled night—
But curtains which thy mercy draws
Between the heavenly world and this?
The terrors of the sea and land—
When all the elements conspire,
The earth and water, ftorm and fire—
Are but the fketches of thy hand;
Do they not all in countless ways—
The lightning's flafh—the howling ftorm—
The dread volcano's awful blaze—
Proclaim thy glory and thy praise?
Beneath the sunny summer fhowers
Thy love affumes a milder form,
And writes its angel name in flowers;
The wind that flies with winged feet
Around the graffy gladden'd earth,
Seems but commiffion'd to repeat
In echo's accents—filvery sweet—

That Thou, O Lord, didſt give it birth.
There is a tongue in every flame—
There is a tongue in every wave—
To these the bounteous Godhead gave
These organs but to praise his name!

LYRA GERMANICA.

LYRA GERMANICA.

FIRST SUNDAY IN ADVENT.

THE night is far spent, the day is at hand; let us therefore cast off the works of darkness, and put on the armor of light.
From the Epistle.

O WATCHMAN will the night of fin
    Be never paft?
O watchman, doth the day begin
To dawn upon thy ftraining fight at laft?
    Will it dispel
Ere long the mifts of sense wherein I dwell?

Now all the earth is bright and glad
    With the frefh morn;
But all my heart is cold, and dark, and sad;
Sun of the soul, let me behold thy dawn!
    Come Jesus, Lord!
Oh, quickly come, according to thy word!

Do we not live in those bleſt days
    So long foretold,
When Thou ſhouldſt come to bring us light and grace?
And yet I ſit in darkness as of old,
    Pining to see
Thy glory; but Thou ſtill art far from me.

Long ſince Thou cam'ſt to be the light
    Of all men here;
And yet in me is nought but blackeſt night.
Wilt Thou not then to me, thine own, appear?
    Shine forth and bless
My soul with viſion of thy righteousness!

If thus in darkness ever left,
    Can I fulfil
The works of light, while of all light bereft?
How ſhall I learn in love and meekness ſtill
    To follow Thee,
And all the ſinful works of darkness flee?

The light of reason cannot give
    Life to my soul;
Jesus alone can make me truly live,
One glance of his can make my spirit whole.
    Arise, and ſhine
On this poor longing, waiting heart of mine!

Single and clear, not weak or blind,
    The eye muſt be,

To which thy glory fhall an entrance find;
For if thy chosen ones would gaze on Thee,
      No earthly screen
Between their souls and Thee muft intervene.

Jesus, do Thou mine eyes unseal,
      And let them grow
Quick to discern whate'er Thou doft reveal,
So fhall I be deliver'd from that woe,
      Blindly to ftray
Through hopeless night, while all around is day.
                                Richter, 1704.

FOURTH SUNDAY IN ADVENT.

Rejoice in the Lord alway, and again I say unto you,
Rejoice . . . The Lord is at hand.
                                    From the Epistle.

LIFT up your heads, ye mighty gates,
    Behold the King of glory waits,
    The King of kings is drawing near,
    The Saviour of the world is here;
Life and salvation doth He bring,
Wherefore rejoice, and gladly fing
    Praise, O my God, to Thee!
    Creator, wise is thy decree!

The Lord is juft, a helper tried,
    Mercy is ever at his fide,
    His Kingly crown is holiness,
    His sceptre, pity in diftress,
The end of all our woe He brings;
Wherefore the earth is glad and fings
    Praise, O my God, to Thee!
    O Saviour, great thy deeds fhall be!

O bleft the land, the city bleft,
    Where Chrift the Ruler is confeft!
    O happy hearts, and happy homes,
    To whom this King in triumph comes!
The cloudless Sun of joy He is,
Who bringeth pure delight and bliss;
    Praise, O my God, to thee!
    Comforter, for thy comfort free!

Fling wide the portals of your heart,
    Make it a temple, set apart
    From earthly use for Heaven's employ,
    Adorn'd with prayer, and love, and joy;
So fhall your Sovereign enter in,
And new and nobler life begin.
    Praise, O my God, be thine,
    For word, and deed, and grace divine.

Redeemer, come! I open wide
    My heart to Thee; here, Lord, abide!
    Let me thy inner presence feel,

Thy grace and love in me reveal,
Thy Holy Spirit guide us on
Until our glorious goal be won!
　　Eternal praise and fame,
　　Be offer'd, Saviour, to thy name!
　　　　　　　　　Weiszel. 1635.

ST. STEPHEN'S DAY.

I HAVE seen, I have seen the afflictions of my people.
　　　　　　　　　　From the Lesson.

FEAR not, O little flock, the foe
　Who madly seek your overthrow,
　　Dread not his rage and power.
What though your courage sometimes faints,
His seeming triumph o'er God's saints
　　Lafts but a little hour.

Be of good cheer; your cause belongs
To Him who can avenge your wrongs
　　Leave it to Him, our Lord.
Though hidden yet from all our eyes,
He sees the Gideon who fhall rise
　　To save us, and his word.

As true as God's own word is true,
Not earth or hell with all their crew
    Againſt us ſhall prevail.
A jeſt and byword are they grown;
God is with us, we are his own,
    Our victory cannot fail.

Amen, Lord Jesus, grant our prayer:
Great Captain, now thine arm make bare;
    Fight for us once again!
So ſhall the saints and martyrs raise
A mighty chorus to thy praise,
    World without end. Amen.
                            Altenburg.
Guſtavus Adolphus's Battle-Song. 1631.

INNOCENTS' DAY.

EXCEPT ye be converted, and become as little children, ye shall not enter into the Kingdom of Heaven. *Matt.* 18 : 3.

DEAR Soul, couldſt thou become a child
While yet on earth, meek, undefiled,
Then God himself were ever near,
And Paradise around thee here.

A child cares nought for gold or treasure,
Nor fame nor glory yield him pleasure;
In perfect truſt, he asketh not
If rich or poor ſhall be his lot.

Little he recks of dignity
Nor prince nor monarch feareth he;
Strange that a child so weak and small
Is oft the boldeſt of us all!

He hath not ſkill to utter lies,
His very soul is in his eyes;
Single his aim in all, and true,
And apt to praise what others do.

No quesſtions dark his spirit vex,
No faithless doubts his soul perplex,
Simply from day to day he lives,
Content with what the present gives.

Scarce can he ſtand alone, far less
Would roam abroad in loneliness;
Faſt clinging to his mother ſtill
She bears and leads him at her will.

He will not ſtay to pause and choose,
His father's guidance e'er refuse,
Thinks not of danger, fears no harm,
Wrapt in obedience' holy calm.

For ſtrange concerns he careth nought;
What others do, although were wrought
Before his eyes the worſt offence,
Stains not his tranquil innocence.

His deareſt work, his beſt delight,
Is, lying in his mother's ſight,
To gaze forever on her face,
And neſtle in her fond embrace.

O childhood's innocence! The voice
Of thy deep wisdom is my choice!
Who hath thy love is truly wise
And precious in our Father's eyes.

Spirit of childhood! loved of God,
By Jesus' spirit now beſtowed;
How often have I long'd for thee;
O Jesus, form thyself in me!

And help me to become a child
While yet on earth, meek, undefiled,
That I may find God always near,
And Paradise around me here.

     Gerhardt Terſteegen. 1731.

THE CIRCUMCISION OF CHRIST.

Hymn for New Year's Day.

So teach us to number our days that we may apply our hearts
unto wisdom.   *Psalm* 90: 12.

ETERNITY! Eternity!
How long art thou, Eternity!
And yet to thee Time haſtes away,
Like as the war-horse to the fray,
Or swift as couriers homeward go,
Or ſhip to port, or ſhaft from bow.
Ponder, O man, Eternity!

Eternity! Eternity!
How long art thou, Eternity!
For even as on a perfect sphere
End nor beginning can appear,

Even so, Eternity, in thee
Entrance nor exit can there be.
Ponder, O man, Eternity!

Eternity! Eternity!
How long art thou, Eternity!
A circle infinite art thou,
Thy centre an Eternal Now,
Never, we name thy outward bound,
For never end therein is found.
Ponder, O man, Eternity!

Eternity! Eternity!
How long art thou, Eternity!
A little bird with fretting beak
Might wear to nought the loftieft peak,
Though but each thousand years it came,
Yet thou wert then, as now, the same.
Ponder, O man, Eternity!

Eternity! Eternity!
How long art thou, Eternity!
As long as God is God, so long
Endure the pains of hell and wrong,
So long the joys of heaven remain;
Oh lafting joy, Oh lafting pain!
Ponder, O man, Eternity!

Eternity! Eternity!
How long art thou, Eternity!

They who lived poor and naked, reſt
With God for ever rich and bleſt,
And love and praise the higheſt good,
In perfect bliss and gladsome mood.
Ponder, O man, Eternity!

Eternity! Eternity!
How long art thou, Eternity!
Who ponders oft on thee is wise,
All fleshly luſts ſhall he despise,
The world finds place with him no more;
The love of vain delights is o'er.
Ponder, O man, Eternity!

Eternity! Eternity!
How long art thou, Eternity!
Who marks thee well would say to God,
Here, judge, burn, smite me with thy rod,
Here, let me all thy juſtice bear,
When time of grace is paſt, then spare!
Ponder, O man, Eternity!

Eternity! Eternity!
How long art thou, Eternity!
Lo, I, Eternity, warn thee,
O man, that oft thou think on me,
The sinner's puniſhment and pain,
To them who love their God, rich gain!
Ponder, O man, Eternity!

Wulffer. 1648.

SECOND SUNDAY AFTER EPIPHANY.

LIFT up your eyes unto the heavens, and look upon the earth beneath ; for the heavens shall vanish away like smoke, and the earth shall wax old like a garment, and the people that dwell therein shall die in like manner; but my salvation shall be for ever, and my righteousness shall not be abolished.

From the Lesson.

GOD liveth ever!
Wherefore, Soul, despair thou never!
Our God is good, in every place
   His love is known, his help is found,
His mighty arm, and tender grace
   Bring good from ills that hem us round.
      Eafier than we think can He
      Turn to joy our agony.
      Soul, remember 'mid thy pains,
      God o'er all for ever reigns.

God liveth ever!
Wherefore, Soul, despair thou never!
Say, fhall He flumber, fhall He fleep,
   Who gave the eye its power to see?
Shall He not hear his children weep
   Who made the ear so wondroufly?
      God is God ; He sees and hears
      All their troubles, all their tears.

Soul, forget not 'mid thy pains,
God o'er all for ever reigns.

God liveth ever!
Wherefore, Soul, despair thou never!
He who can earth and heaven control,
Who spreads the clouds o'er sea and land,
Whose presence fills the mighty Whole
In each true heart is close at hand.
Love Him, He will surely send
Help and joy that never end.
Soul, remember in thy pains,
God o'er all for ever reigns.

God liveth ever!
Wherefore, Soul, despair thou never.
Scarce canft thou bear thy cross? Then fly
To Him where only reft is sweet;
Thy God is great, his mercy nigh
His ftrength upholds the tottering feet.
Truft Him, for his grace is sure,
Ever doth his truth endure;
Soul, forget not in thy pains,
God o'er all for ever reigns.

God liveth ever!
O my Soul, despair thou never!
When fins and follies long forgot
Upon thy tortured conscience prey,
O come to God, and fear Him not,

His love fhall sweep them all away.
Pains of hell at look of his,
Change to calm content and bliss.
Soul, forget not in thy pain,
God o'er all doth ever reign.

God liveth ever!
Wherefore, Soul, despair thou never!
Those whom the thoughtless world forsakes,
Who ftand bewilder'd with their woe,
God gently to his bosom takes,
And bids them all his fulness know.
In thy sorrows' swelling flood
Own his hand who seeks thy good.
Soul, forget not in thy pains,
God o'er all for ever reigns.

God liveth ever!
Wherefore, Soul, despair thou never!
Let earth and heaven outworn with age,
Sink to the chaos whence they came;
Let angry foes againft us rage,
Let hell fhoot forth his fierceft flame;
Fear not Death, nor Satan's thrufts,
God defends who in Him trufts;
Soul, remember in thy pains,
God o'er all for ever reigns.

God liveth ever!
Wherefore, Soul, despair thou, never!

What though thou tread with bleeding feet
A thorny path of grief and gloom,
Thy God will choose the way moft meet
To lead thee heavenwards, lead thee home.
For this life's long night of sadness
He will give thee peace and gladness.
Soul, forget not in thy pains,
God o'er all for ever reigns.
                        Zihn. 1682.

THIRD SUNDAY AFTER EPIPHANY.

For as the rain cometh down, and the snow from heaven; and returneth not thither, but watereth the earth, and maketh it bring forth and bud, that it may give seed to the sower, and bread to the eater: so shall my word be that goeth forth out of my mouth: it shall not return unto me void, but it shall accomplish that which I please, and it shall prosper in the thing whereto I sent it.
                                From the Lesson.

THY Word, O Lord, like gentle dews,
   Falls soft on hearts that pine;
Lord, to thy garden ne'er refuse
   This heavenly balm of thine.
      Water'd from Thee
      Let every tree
Bud forth and bloffom to thy praise,
And bear much fruit in after days.

Thy Word is like a flaming sword,
   A wedge that cleaveth ſtone;
Keen as a fire so burns thy Word
And pierceth fleſh and bone.
      Let it go forth
      O'er all the earth
To purify all hearts within
And ſhatter all the might of sin.

Thy Word a wondrous guiding ſtar,
   On pilgrim hearts doth rise,
Leads to their Lord who dwell afar,
   And makes the ſimple wise.
      Let not its light
      E'er ſink in night,
But ſtill in every spirit ſhine,
That none may miss thy light divine.

Anon.

QUINQUAGESIMA SUNDAY.

AND Jesus said unto him, Receive thy sight, thy faith hath saved thee: and immediately he received his sight, and followed him, glorifying God. *From the Gospel.*

MY Saviour, what Thou didſt of old
 When Thou waſt dwelling here,
Thou doeſt yet for them, who, bold
 In faith, to Thee draw near.
As Thou hadſt pity on the blind,
 According to thy Word,
Thou ſufferedſt me thy grace to find,
 Thy Light haſt on me pour'd.

Mourning I sat beſide the way,
 In ſightless gloom apart,
And sadness heavy on me lay,
 And longing gnaw'd my heart;
I heard the muſic of the psalms
 Thy people sang to Thee,
I felt the waving of their palms,
 And yet I could not see.

My pain grew more than I could bear,
 Too keen my grief became,
Then I took heart in my despair
 To call upon thy name;
"O Son of David, save and heal,
 As Thou so oft haſt done!

O dearest Jesus, let me feel
    My load of darkness gone."

And ever weeping as I spoke
    With bitter prayers and sighs,
My stony heart grew soft and broke,
    More earnest yet my cries.
A sudden answer still'd my fear,
    For it was said to me,
" O poor blind man, be of good cheer,
    Rejoice, He calleth thee."

I felt, Lord, that Thou stoodest still,
    Groping thy feet I sought,
From off me fell my old self-will,
    A change came o'er my thought.
Thou saidst, " What is it Thou wouldst have ? "
    " Lord, that I might have sight;
To see thy countenance I crave : "
    " So be it, have thou Light."

And words of thine can never fail,
    My fears are past and o'er;
My soul is glad with light, the veil
    Is on my heart no more.
Thou blessest me, and forth I fare
    Free from my old disgrace,
And follow on with joy where'er
    Thy footsteps, Lord, I trace.
                De La Motte Fouque.

SECOND SUNDAY IN LENT.

AND the disciples said, Send her away, for she crieth after us;
.... But he said, Great is thy faith, be it unto thee even as
thou wilt. *From the Gospel.*

I WILL not let Thee go; Thou Help in time of need!
      Heap ill on ill
      I truſt Thee ſtill,
E'en when it seems as Thou wouldſt ſlay indeed!
      Do as Thou wilt with me,
      I yet will cling to Thee,
Hide Thou thy face, yet, Help in time of need,
      I will not let Thee go!

I will not let Thee go; ſhould I forsake my bliss?
      No, Lord, thou'rt mine,
      And I am thine,
Thee will I hold when all things else I miss.
      Though dark and sad the night,
      Joy cometh with thy light,
O Thou my Sun; ſhould I forsake my bliss?
      I will not let Thee go!

I will not let Thee go, my God, my Life, my Lord!
      Not Death can tear
      Me from his care,
Who for my sake his soul in death outpour'd.

Thou diedst for love to me,
I say in love to Thee,
E'en when my heart shall break, my God, my Life, my Lord,
I will not let Thee go!
Deszler. 1692.

THIRD SUNDAY AFTER EASTER.

AND ye now therefore have sorrow; but I will see you again, and your heart shall rejoice, and your joy no man taketh from you. *From the Gospel.*

COMETH sunshine after rain,
After mourning joy again,
After heavy bitter grief
Dawneth surely sweet relief;
 And my soul, who from her height
 Sank to realms of woe and night,
 Wingeth now to heaven her flight.

He, whom this world dares not face,
Hath refresh'd me with his grace,
And his mighty hand unbound
Chains of hell about me wound;

Quicker, stronger, leaps my blood,
Since his mercy, like a flood,
Pour'd o'er all my heart for good.

Bitter anguish have I borne
Keen regret my heart hath torn,
Sorrow dimm'd my weeping eyes,
Satan blinded me with lies;
    Yet at last am I set free,
    Help, protection, love, to me
    Once more true companions be.

Ne'er was left a helpless prey,
Ne'er with shame was turn'd away,
He who gave himself to God,
And on Him had cast a load.
    Who in God his hope hath placed
    Shall not life in pain outwaste,
    Fullest joy he yet shall taste.

Though to-day may not fulfil
All thy hopes, have patience still;
For perchance to-morrow's sun
Sees thy happier days begun.
    As God willeth march the hours,
    Bringing joy at last in showers,
    And whate'er we asked is ours.

When my heart was vex'd with care,
Fill'd with fears, well-nigh despair;

When with watching many a night
On me fell pale ſickneſs' blight;
　When my courage fail'd me faſt,
　Cameſt Thou, my God, at laſt,
　And my woes were quickly paſt.

Now as long as here I roam,
On this earth have house and home,
Shall this wondrous gleam from Thee
Shine through all my memory.
　To my God I yet will cling,
　All my life the praises ſing
　That from thankful hearts outspring.

Every sorrow, every smart,
That the Eternal Father's heart
Hath appointed me of yore,
Or hath yet for me in ſtore,
　As my life flows on I'll take
　Calmly, gladly for his sake,
　No more faithless murmurs make.

I will meet diſtress and pain,
I will greet e'en death's dark reign,
I will lay me in the grave,
With a heart ſtill glad and brave.
　Whom the Strongeſt doth defend,
　Whom the Higheſt counts his friend,
　Cannot periſh in the end.
　　　　　　　Paul Gerhardt. 1659.

FOURTH SUNDAY AFTER EASTER.

IT is expedient for you that I go away, for if I go not away, the Comforter will not come unto you.
From the Gospel.

O HOLY Ghoſt! Thou fire Divine!
From higheſt heaven on us down ſhine;
Comforter, be thy comfort mine!

Come, Father of the poor, to earth;
Come with thy gifts of precious worth;
Come, Light of all of mortal birth!

Thou rich in comfort! Ever bleſt
The heart where Thou art conſtant gueſt,
Who giv'ſt the heavy-laden reſt.

Come, Thou in whom our toil is sweet,
Our ſhadow in the noon-day heat,
Before whom mourning flieth fleet.

Bright Sun of Grace! Thy sunſhine dart
On all who cry to Thee apart,
And fill with gladness every heart.

Whate'er without thy aid is wrought,
Or skilful deed or wisest thought,
God counts it vain and merely nought.

O cleanse us that we sin no more,
O'er parched souls thy waters pour;
Heal the sad heart that acheth sore.

Thy will be ours in all our ways;
O melt the frozen with thy rays;
Call home the lost in error's maze.

And grant us, Lord, who cry to Thee,
And hold the faith in unity,
Thy precious gifts of charity;

That we may live in holiness,
And find in death our happiness,
And dwell with Thee in lasting bliss.
  King Robert of France about A. D. 1000.

TRINITY SUNDAY.

AND God said, Let us make man in our image.
From the Lesson.

MOST High and Holy Trinity!
Who of thy mercy mild
Haft form'd me here in time, to be
　Thy image and thy child :
Oh let me love Thee day and night
With all my soul, with all my might;
Oh come, thyself my soul prepare,
And make thy dwelling ever there!

Father! replenifh with thy grace
　This longing heart of mine,
Make it thy quiet dwelling-place,
　Thy sacred inmoft fhrine!
Forgive that oft my spirit wears
Her time and ftrength in trivial cares,
Enfold her in thy changeless peace,
So fhe from all but Thee may cease!

O God the Son! thy wisdom's light
　On my dark reason pour;
Forgive that things of sense and fight,
　Were all her joy of yore;

Henceforth let every thought and deed
On Thee be fix'd, from Thee proceed,
Draw me to Thee, for I would rise
Above these earthly vanities!

O, Holy Ghoft! Thou fire of love,
   Enkindle with thy flame my will;
Come, with thy ftrength, Lord, from above,
   Help me thy bidding to fulfil :
Forgive that I so oft have done
What I as finful ought to fhun;
Let me with pure and quenchless fire
Thy favor and thyself defire!

Moft High and Holy Trinity!
   Draw me away far hence,
And fix upon eternity
   All powers of soul and sense!
Make me at one within; at one
With Thee on earth; when life is done
Take me to dwell in light with Thee,
Moft High and Holy Trinity!
Angelus. 1657.

THIRD SUNDAY AFTER TRINITY.

CAST all your care upon Him, for He careth for you.
From the Epistle.

GOD! Thou art my Rock of ftrength,
    And my home is in thine arms,
Thou wilt send me help at length,
    And I feel no wild alarms.
Sin nor Death can pierce the fhield
    Thy defence has o'er me thrown,
Up to Thee myfelf I yield,
    And my sorrows are thine own.

On Thee, O my God, I reft,
    Letting life float calmly on,
For I know the laft is beft,
    When the crown of joy is won.
In thy might all things I bear,
    In thy love find bitters sweet,
And with all my grief and care
    Sit in patience at thy feet.

O, my soul, why art thou vex'd?
    Let things go e'en as they will;
Though to thee they seem perplex'd
    Yet his order they fulfil.
Here He is thy ftrength and guard,
    Power to harm thee here has none;

Yonder will He each reward
For the works he here has done.

Let thy mercy's wings be spread
  O'er me, keep me close to Thee,
In the peace thy love doth shed,
  Let me dwell eternally.
Be my All; in all I do
  Let me only seek thy will,
Where the heart to Thee is true,
  All is peaceful, calm, and still.
                A. H. Francke. 1663–1727.

NINTH SUNDAY AFTER TRINITY.

How long halt ye between two opinions? If the Lord be God, follow him: but if Baal, then follow him.
                          From the Lesson.

WHY halteft thus, deluded heart,
  Why waverest longer in thy choice?
Is it so hard to choose the part
  Offer'd by Heaven's entreating voice?
Oh look with clearer eyes again,
Nor ftrive to enter in, in vain.
        Press on!

Remember, 'tis not Cæsar's throne,
  Nor earthly honor, wealth, or might,

Whereby God's favor shall be shown
 To him who conquers in this fight;
Himself and an eternity
Of bliss and rest He offers thee.
                    Press on!

Then break the rotten bonds away,
 That hinder you your race to run,
That make you linger oft and stay;
 Oh, be your course afresh begun!
Let no false rest your soul deceive,
Up! 'tis a Heaven ye must achieve!
                    Press on!

Omnipotence is on your side,
 And wisdom watches o'er your heads,
And God himself will be your guide
 So ye but follow where He leads;
How many guided by his hand,
Have reach'd ere now their native land.
                    Press on!

Let not the body dull the soul,
 Its weakness, fears, and sloth despise;
Man toils and roams from pole to pole
 To gain some earthly fleeting prize,
The highest good he little cares
To win, or striving soon despairs.
                    Press on!

Oh, help each other, haften on,
 Behold the goal is nigh at hand;
Soon fhall the battle-field be won,
 Soon fhall your King before you ftand!
To calmeft reft He leads you now,
And sets his crown upon your brow.
 Press on!
 Lehr. 1733.

ELEVENTH SUNDAY AFTER TRINITY.

In thy presence is fulness of joy; at thy right hand there are pleasures for evermore. *Psalm* 16 : 11.

O FRIEND of souls, how well is me
 Whene'er thy love my spirit calms!
From sorrow's dungeon forth I flee
 And hide me in thy fhelt'ring arms.
The night of weeping flies away
Before the heat-reviving ray
 Of love, that beams from out thy breaft;
Here is my heaven on earth begun;
Who were not joyful had he won
 In Thee, O God, his joy and reft!

The world may call herself my foe,
 So be it; for I truft her not,

E'en though a friendly face she show,
    And heap with her good things my lot.
In Thee alone will I rejoice,
Thou art the Friend, Lord, of my choice,
    For Thou art true when friendships fail;
'Mid storms of woe thy truth is still
My anchor; hate me as it will,
    The world shall o'er me ne'er prevail.

Through deserts of the cross Thou leadest,
    I follow leaning on thy hand;
From out the clouds thy child Thou feedest,
    And giv'st him water from the sand.
I know thy wondrous ways will end
In love and blessing, Thou true Friend,
    Enough if Thou art ever near!
I know, whom Thou wilt glorify,
And raise o'er sun and stars on high,
    Thou lead'st through depths and darkness here.
                             Deszler. 1692.

THIRTEENTH SUNDAY AFTER TRINITY.

THEN Hezekiah received the letter at the hands of the messenger, and read it, and Hezekiah went up into the house of the Lord, and spread it before the Lord. *From the Lesson.*

LEAVE God to order all thy ways,
   And hope in Him whate'er betide,
Thou'lt find Him in the evil days
   Thy all-sufficient ftrength and guide;
Who trufts in God's unchanging love,
Builds on the rock that nought can move.

What can these anxious cares avail
   These never-ceafing moans and fighs?
What can it help us to bewail
   Each painful moment as it flies?
Our cross and trials do but press
The heavier for our bitterness.

Only thy reftless heart keep ftill,
   And wait in cheerful hope; content
To take whate'er his gracious will,
   His all-discerning love hath sent.
Doubt not our inmoft wants are known
To Him who chose us for his own.

He knows when joyful hours are beft,
    He sends them as He sees it meet;
When thou haft borne the fiery teft,
    And art made free from all deceit,
He comes to thee all unaware
And makes thee own his loving care.

Nor in the heat of pain and ftrife,
    Think God hath caft thee off unheard,
And that the man, whose prosperous life
    Thou envieft, is of Him preferr'd.
Time paffes and much change doth bring,
And sets a bound to every thing.

All are alike before his face;
    'Tis easy to our God moft High
To make the rich man poor and base,
    To give the poor man wealth and joy.
True wonders ftill by Him are wrought,
Who setteth up, and brings to nought.

Sing, pray, and swerve not from his ways,
    But do thine own part faithfully,
Truft his rich promises of grace
    So fhall they be fulfill'd in thee;
God never yet forsook at need
The soul that trufted Him indeed.
                  Neumarck. 1653.

MORNING HYMN.

COME, my soul, awake, 'tis morning,
    Day is dawning
O'er the earth, arise and pray;
Come, to Him who made this splendor,
    Thou muſt render
All thy feeble powers can pay.

From the ſtars now learn thy duty,
    See their beauty
Paling in the golden air;
So God's light thy miſts ſhould baniſh,
    Thus ſhould vaniſh
What to darken'd sense seem'd fair.

See how every thing that liveth,
    Gladly ſtriveth
On the pleasant light to gaze;
Stirs with joy each thing that groweth,
    As it knoweth
Darkness smitten by its rays.

Soul, thy incense also proffer;
    Thou ſhouldſt offer
Praise to Him, who from thy head

Kept afar the storms of sorrow,
      That the morrow
Finds the night in peace hath fled.

Bid Him bless what thou art doing,
      If pursuing
Some good aim; but if there lurks
Ill intent in thine endeavor,
      May He ever
Thwart and turn thee from thy works.

Think that He, the all-discerning,
      Knows each turning
Of thy path, each sinful stain;
Nay, what shame would fain gloss over,
      Can discover;
All thou dost to Him is plain.

Bound unto the flying hours
      Are our powers;
Earth's vain good floats down their wave,
That thy ship, my soul, is hasting,
      Never resting,
To its haven in the grave.

Pray that when thy life is closing,
      Calm reposing,
Thou mayst die, and not in pain;
That the night of death departed,

Thou glad-hearted,
Mayſt behold the Sun again.

From God's glances ſhrink thou never,
        Meet them ever;
Who submits him to his grace,
Finds that earth no sunſhine knoweth
        Such as gloweth
O'er his pathway all his days.

Waken'ſt thou again to sorrow,
        Oh! then borrow
Strength from Him, whose sun-like might
On the mountain-summit tarries,
        And yet carries
To the vales their mirth and light.

Round the gifts He on thee ſhowers,
        Fiery towers
Will He set, be not afraid;
Thou ſhalt dwell 'mid angel-legions,
        In the regions
Satan's self dares not invade.
                Von Canitz. 1654–1699.

FOR THE SICK AND DYING.

GOD! whom I as Love have known,
Thou haſt ſickneſs laid on me,
   And these pains are sent of Thee,
Under which I burn and moan;
Let them burn away the ſin,
   That too oft hath check'd the love
   Wherewith Thou my heart wouldſt move,
When thy Spirit works within!

In my weakness be Thou ſtrong,
   Be Thou sweet when I am sad,
   Let me ſtill in Thee be glad,
Though my pains be keen and long.
All that plagues my body now,
   All that waſteth me away,
   Preſſing on me night and day,
Love hath sent, for Love art Thou!

Suffering is the work now sent,
   Nothing can I do but lie
   Suffering as the hours go by;
All my powers to this are bent.
Suffering is my gain; I bow
   To my heavenly Father's will
   And receive it huſh'd and ſtill;
Suffering is my worſhip now.

Richter, 1713.

FOR THE BURIAL OF THE DEAD.

NOW rests her soul in Jesus' arms,
    Her body in the grave sleeps well,
His heart her death-chill'd heart rewarms,
    And rest more deep than tongue can tell,—
Her few brief hours of conflict pass'd,—
She finds with Christ, her Friend, at last;
She bathes in tranquil seas of peace,
    God wipes away her tears, she feels
    New life that all her languor heals,
The glory of the Lamb she sees.

She hath escaped all danger now,
    Her pain and sighing all are fled;
The crown of joy is on her brow,
    Eternal glories o'er her shed,
In golden robes, a queen, a bride,
She standeth at her Sovereign's side,
She sees his face unveil'd and bright;
    With joy and love He greets her soul
    She sees herself made inly whole,
A lesser light amid his light.

The child hath now its Father seen,
    And feels what kindling love may be,
And knoweth what those words may mean,
    "Himself, the Father, loveth thee."

A shoreless ocean, an abyss
Unfathom'd, fill'd with good and bliss,
Now breaks on her enraptured sight;
    She sees God's face, she learneth there
    What this shall be, to be his heir,
Joint heir with Christ her Lord, in light.
Allendorf, 1725.

L

LYRA APOSTOLICA.

LYRA APOSTOLICA.

HOLINESS.

"The effectual fervent prayer of a righteous man availeth much."

THERE is not on the earth a soul so base
    But may obtain a place
    In covenanted grace ;
So that forthwith his prayer of faith obtains
    Release of his guilt-ſtains,
And firſt-fruits of the second birth, which rise
From gift to gift, and reach at length the eternal prize.

All may save self ;—but minds that heavenward tower,
    Aim at a wider power,
    Gifts on the world to ſhower.—
And this is not at once ;—by faſtings gained,
    And trials well suſtained,
By pureness, righteous deeds, and toils of love,
Abidance in the truth, and zeal for God above.

AFFLICTION.

"THOU in faithfulness hast afflicted me."

LORD, in this duft thy sovereign voice
   Firft quickened love divine ;
I am all thine,—thy care and choice,
   My very praise is thine.

I praise Thee, while thy providence
   In childhood frail I trace,
For bleffings given, ere dawning sense
   Could seek or scan thy grace ;

Bleffings in boyhood's marvelling hour
   Bright dreams, and fancyings ftrange ;
Bleffings, when reason's awful power
   Gave thought a bolder range ;

Bleffings of friends, which to my door
   Unafked, unhoped, have come ;
And, choicer ftill, a countless ftore
   Of eager smiles at home.

Yet, Lord, in memory's fondeft place
   I fhrine those seasons sad,
When, looking up, I saw thy face
   In kind auftereness clad.

I would not miss one sigh or tear
    Heart-pang or throbbing brow;
Sweet was the chastisement severe,
    And sweet its memory now.

Yes! let the fragrant scars abide,
    Love-tokens in thy stead,
Faint shadows of the spear-pierced side,
    And thorn-encompassed head.

And such thy loving force be still,
    'Mid life's fierce shifting fray,
Shaping to Truth self's froward will
    Along thy narrow way.

Deny me wealth; far, far remove
    The lure of power or name;
Hope thrives in straits, in weakness Love,
    And Faith in this world's shame.

DISCIPLINE.

WHEN I look back upon my former race,
    Seasons I see, at which the Inward Ray
More brightly burned, or guided some new way;
Truth, in its wealthier scene and nobler space,
Given for my eye to range, and feet to trace,
    And next I mark, 'twas trial did convey,
    Or grief, or pain, or strange eventful day,
To my tormented soul such larger grace.
So now, whene'er, in journeying on, I feel
The shadow of the Providential Hand,
Deep breathless stirrings shoot across my breast,
Searching to know what He will now reveal,
What sin uncloak, what stricter rule command,
And girding me to work his full behest.

LEAD THOU ME ON.

SHED kindly light amid the encircling gloom
    And lead me on!
The night is dark, and I am far from home,
    Lead Thou me on!
Keep Thou my feet: I do not ask to see
The *distant* scene: one step enough for me.

I was not ever thus, nor prayed that Thou
    Should'st lead me on!
I loved to choose and see my path, but now
    Lead Thou me on!
I loved day's dazzling light, and spite of fears
Pride ruled my will; remember not past years!

So long thy power hath blessed me, surely still
    'Twill lead me on!
Through dreary doubt, through pain and sorrow till
    The night is gone.
And with the morn those angel faces smile
Which I have loved long since, and lost awhile.

DEEDS NOT WORDS.

PRUNE thou thy words, the thoughts control
    That o'er thee swell and throng;
They will condense within thy soul
    And change to purpose strong.

But he, who lets his feelings run
    In soft luxurious flow,
Shrinks when hard service must be done,
    And faints at every woe.

Faith's meaneſt deed more favour bears,
  Where hearts and wills are weighed,
Than brighteſt transports, choiceſt prayers,
  Which bloom their hour and fade.

HOLINESS.

" Be strong, and He shall comfort thine heart."

" LORD, I have faſted, I have prayed,
    And sackcloth has my girdle been,
To purge my soul I have eſſayed
    With hunger blank and vigil keen.
O God of mercy! why am I
Still haunted by the self I fly?"

Sackcloth is a girdle good,
    O bind it round thee ſtill;
Faſting, it is angels' food,
    And Jesus loved the night-air chill;
Yet think not prayer and faſt were given
To make one ſtep 'twixt earth and heaven.

DAVID AND JONATHAN.

"THY love to me was wonderful, passing the love of women."

O HEART of fire! misjudged by wilful man,
    Thou flower of Jesse's race!
What woe was thine, when thou and Jonathan
    Last greeted face to face!
He doom'd to die, thou on us to impress
The portent of a blood-stained holiness.

Yet it was well :—for so, mid cares of rule,
    And crime's encircling tide,
A spell was o'er thee, zealous one, to cool
    Earth-joy and kingly pride;
With battle-scene and pageant, prompt to blend
The pale calm sceptre of a blameless friend.

Ah! had he lived, before thy throne to stand
    Thy spirit keen and high,
Sure it had snapped in twain love's slender band,
    So dear in memory;
Paul's strife unblest,* its serious lesson gives,
He bides with us who dies, he is but lost who lives.

* Acts 15 : 39.

BEREAVEMENT.

"WHEREFORE I abhor myself, and repent in duſt and ashes."
    JOB xlii. 6.

AND dare I say, "welcome to me
　　The pang that proves thee near?"
O words, too oft on bended knee
　　Breathed to the Unerring Ear.
While the cold spirit ſilently
　　Pines at the scourge severe.

Nay, try once more—thine eyelids close
　　For prayer intense and meek:
When the warm light gleams through and ſhows
　　Him near who helps the weak.
Unmurmuring then thy heart's repose
　　In duſt and aſhes seek.

But when the self-abhorring thrill
　　Is paſt, as pass it muſt,
When tasks of life thy spirit fill,
　　Risen from thy tears and duſt,
Then be the self-renouncing will
　　The seal of thy calm truſt.

CONFESSION.

MY smile is bright, my glance is free,
    My voice is calm and clear;
Dear friend, I seem a type to thee
    Of holy love and fear.

But I am scanned by eyes unseen,
    And these no saint surround;
They mete what is, by what has been,
    And joy the loſt is found.

Erst my good Angel ſhrank to see
    My thoughts and ways of ill;
And now he scarce dare gaze on me,
    Scar-seamed and crippled ſtill.

FAITH.

" It is I: be not afraid."

WHEN I sink down in gloom or fear,
    Hope blighted or delayed,
Thy whisper, Lord, my heart shall cheer
    " 'Tis I : be not afraid ! "

Or, startled at some sudden blow,
    If fretful thoughts I feel,
"Fear not, it is but I ! " shall flow
    As balm my wound to heal.

Nor will I quit thy way, though foes
    Some onward pass defend ;
From each rough voice the watchword goes,
    " Be not afraid ! . . . a friend ! "

And O ! when judgment's trumpet clear
    Awakes me from the grave,
Still in its echo may I hear,
    " 'Tis Christ ! He comes to save."

HOME.

BANISHED the House of sacred rest
    Amid a thoughtless throng,
At length I heard its Creed confessed,
    And knelt the Saints among.

Artless his strain and unadorned,
    Who spoke Christ's message there;
But what at home I might have scorned,
    Now charmed my famished ear.

Lord, grant me this abiding grace,
    Thy Word and Sons to know;
To pierce the veil on Moses' face,
    Although his speech be slow!

LYRA INNOCENTIUM.

M

LYRA INNOCENTIUM.

UNWEARIED LOVE.

"JESUS saith unto him, I say not unto thee, until seven times; but until seventy times seven."

MY child, the counsels high attend
   Of thine Eternal Friend.
When longings pure, when holy prayers,
When self-denying thoughts and cares
   Room in thy heart would win,
Stay not too long to count them o'er;
Rise in His name; throw wide the door,
   Let the good Angels in:

Nor liften, fhould the Tempter say,
   "How wearying, day by day,
To say the prayer we said before,
The mountain path climb o'er and o'er,
   No end to warfare find!"

Nor seek thou limit to discern
In patient woe, in duty ſtern,
  But learn thy (Saviour's) mind.

He pardoning wearies not. Ah why
  Behold with evil eye
Thy brother aſking grace for ſin?
He doth but aid thee, more to win
  Of hope in thy laſt end.
In heart forgive—that pays Him all:
But grudging souls muſt die in thrall,
  No Saviour and no Friend.

THE BOY WITH THE FIVE LOAVES.

"IF thou hast little, do thy diligence gladly to give of that little."

WHAT time the Saviour spread his feaſt
  For thousands on the mountain's ſide,
One of the laſt and leaſt
  The abundant store supplied.

Haply the wonders to behold,
  A boy, 'mid other boys he came,
A lamb of Jesus' fold,
  Though now unknown by name.

Or for his sweet obedient ways
  The Apostles brought him near, to share
  Their Lord's laborious days,
    His frugal basket bear.

Or might it be his duteous heart
  That led him sacrifice to bring
  For his own simple part,
    To the world's hidden King?

Well may I guess how glow'd his cheek,
  How he look'd down, half pride, half fear:
  Far off he saw one speak
    Of him in JESUS' ear.

" There is a lad—five loaves hath he,
  And fishes twain—but what are they,
  Where hungry thousands be ? "
    Nay, Christ will find a way.

In order, on the fresh green hill,
  The mighty Shepherd ranks his sheep
  By tens and fifties, still
    As clouds when breezes sleep.

Or who can tell the trembling joy,
  Who paint the grave endearing look,
  When from that favored boy
    The wondrous pledge He took?—

Keep thou, dear child, thine early word ;
Bring Him thy beſt : who knows but He
For his eternal board
May take some gift of thee ?

Thou prayeſt without the veil as yet :
But kneel in faith : an arm benign
Such prayers will duly set
Within the holieſt ſhrine.

And Prayer has might to spread and grow.
Thy childiſh darts, right-aim'd on high,
May catch Heaven's fire, and glow
Far in the eternal ſky :

Even as He made that ſtripling's ſtore
Type of the feaſt by Him decreed,
Where Angels might adore,
And souls for ever feed.

HEZEKIAH'S DISPLAY.

" There is nothing among my treasures that I have not showed them."

WHEN Heaven in mercy gives thy prayers return,
 And Angels bring thee treasures from on high,
Shut fast the door, nor let the world discern,
 And offer thee fond praise when God is nigh.

In friendly guise, perchance with friendly heart,
 From Babel, see, they haſte with words of love:
But if thou lightly all thy wealth impart,
 Their race will come again, and all remove.

Ill thoughts, the children of that King of Pride,
 O'er richeſt halls will swarm, and holieſt bowers,
Profaning firſt, then spoiling far and wide:
 Voluptuous Sloth make free with Sharon's flowers.

Close thou the garden-gate, and keep the key,
 There chiefly, where the tender seedlings fold
Their dainty leaves—a treasure even to thee
 Unknown, till air celeſtial make them bold.

When sun and ſhower give token, freely then
 The fragrance will ſteal out, the flower unclose:

But busy hands, and an admiring ken,
Have blighted ere its hour full many a rose.

Then reft thee, bright one, in thy tranquil nook,
Fond eyes to cherifh thee, true arms to keep,
Nor wiftful for the world's gay sunfhine look;—
In its own time the light will o'er thee sweep.

FINE CLOTHES.

"AND a very great multitude spread their garments in the way; others cut down branches from the trees, and strewed them in the way."

(For Palm Sunday.)

LOOK weftward, penfive little one,
How the bright hues together run,
Around where late the waning sun
  Sank in his evening cloud.
Or eaftward turn thee, and admire
How linger yet the fhowers of fire,
Deep in each fold, high on each spire
  Of yonder mountain proud.

Thou seeft it not: an envious screen,
A fluttering leaflet, hangs between

Thee and that fair myſterious scene,
 A veil too near thine eye.
One finger's breadth at hand will mar
A world of light in heaven afar,
A mote eclipse a glorious ſtar,
 An eyelid hide the ſky.

And while to clear the view we ſtay
Lo! the bright hour hath paſſ'd away;
A twilight haze, all dim and gray,
 Hath quench'd the living gleam.
Remember this, thou little child,
In hours of prayer, when fancies wild
Betwixt thee and thy Saviour mild
 Come floating on life's ſtream.

O ſhame, O grief, when earth's rude toys,
An opening door, a breath, a noise,
Drive from the heart th' eternal joys,
 Displace the Lord of Love!
For half a prayer perchance on high
We soar, and heaven seems bright and nigh,
But ah! too soon frail heart and eye
 Sink down and earthward rove.

The Sunday garment glittering gay
The Sunday heart will ſteal away.
Then haſte thee, ere the fond glance ſtray,
 Thy precious robes unfold,

And caſt before thy Saviour's feet:
Him spare not with thy beſt to greet,
Nor dread the duſt of Sion's ſtreet,
   'Tis jewels all and gold.

SHYNESS.

"Moses hid his face; for he was afraid to look upon God."

TEAR not away the veil, dear friend,
   Nor from its ſhelter rudely rend
     The heaven-protected flower:
     It waits for sun and ſhower
To woo it kindly forth in its own time,
And when they come, untaught will know its hour of prime.

Blame not the eye that from thee turns,
   The cheek that in a moment burns
     With tingling fire so bright,
     Feeling thine eager ſight,—
The lowly drooping brow, the ſtammering tongue,
The giddy wavering thought, scarce knowing right and wrong.

With quivering hands that closely fold
Over his downcaſt eyes, behold
   The Shepherd on the Mount
   Adores the Living Fount
Of pure unwaſting fire: no glance he ſteals,
But in his heart's deep joy the Dread Eye gazing feels,—

Feels it, and gladlier far would die
Than let it go. There will he lie
   Till the Dread Voice return,
   And he the lore may learn
Of his appointed taſk—bold deeds to dare,
High myſteries to impart, deep penances to bear.

Then tear we not the veil away,
Nor ruthless tell in open day
   The tender spirit's dream.
   O let the deepening ſtream,
Might, from the mountain-springs in ſilence draw;
O mar we nbt his work, who trains his saints in awe.

THE GLEANERS.

THE Church is one wide harveſt field,
   Where Time and Death are gathering in
Rich bleſſings by the Almighty owner sealed
   For spirits meet his pardoning word to win.

We are as children : here and there
   A few fallen ears, the ſheaves among,
We glean, where beſt the bounteous Hand may spare,
   So learning for his perfeƈt ſtore to long.

Come, little ones—come early out,
   Come joyous, come with ſteady heart,
Roam not to seek wild flowers the field about,
   Nor yet at dreams of fancied vipers ſtart.

The sun of Autumn climbs full faſt :
   He will have quaffed each drop of dew,
Ere half the fragrant, healthy lane be paſſed,
   The lingerers, they will find scant ears and few.

Come, quit your toys, and haſte away.
   But mark : ye may not leave behind
Your ſtore of smiles, your gladsome talk and gay,
   Your pure thoughts, faſhioned to your Maſter's mind.

Blithe be your course, yet bear in heart
  The lame and old, and help them on;
Full handfulls drop where they may take a part,
  As high will swell your heap when day is done.

Yon flumbering infant in the fhade,—
  Grudge not one hour on him to wait
While others glean. The work with finging aid,
  With ready mirth all fharper tones abate.

Sing softly in your heart all day
  Sweet carols to the harveft's Lord,
So fhall ye chase those evil powers away
  That walk at noon—rude gaze and wanton word.

EFFECT OF EXAMPLE.

"FOR I have five brethren; that he may testify unto them, lest they also come into this place of torment."

FIVE loving souls, each one as mine,
  And each for evermore to be!
  Each deed of each to thrill
    For good or ill
  Along thine awful line,
    Eternity!

Who for such burden may suffice?
Who bear to think, how scornful tone,
　Or word or glance too bold,
　Or ill dream told,
May bar from Paradise
Our Master's own?

We scatter seeds with careless hand,
And dream we ne'er shall see them more:
　But for a thousand years
　Their fruit appears,
In weeds that mar the land,
Or healthful store.

The deeds we do, the words we say,—
Into still air they seem to fleet,
　We count them ever past;
　But they shall last,
In the dread judgment they
And we shall meet!

I charge thee by the years gone by,
For the love's sake of brethren dear,
　Keep thou the one true way
　In work and play,
Lest in that world their cry
Of woe thou hear!

THE WATERFALL.

"Ye also, as lively stones, are built up, a spiritual house."
"I will make thy seed as the dust of the earth."

" WHAT is the Church, and what am I?
    A world, to one poor sandy grain,
      A wafte of sea and fky
    To one frail drop of rain.

"What boots one feeble infant tone
    To the full choir denied or given,
      Where millions round the Throne
    Are chanting, morn and even?"

Nay, the kind Watchers hearkening there
    Diftinguifh in the deep of song
      Each little wave, each air
    Upon the faltering tongue.

Each half note in the great Amen,
    Even by the utterer's self unheard,
      They ftore: O fail not then
    To bring thy lowly word:

Spare not to swell the bold acclaim;
    So in the future battle-fhout,
      When at the Saviour's name
    The Church fhall call thee out,

No doubtful sound thy trump ſhall pour.
Remember, when in earlier days
   Thou toil'dſt upon the floor
     Palace or tower to raise,

No mimic ſtone but found a place,
And glorious to the builder ſhone
   The pile: then how ſhould Grace
     One living gem disown,

One pearly mote, one diamond small,
One sparkle of th' unearthly light?—
   Go where the waters fall
     Sheer from the mountains height;·

Mark how, a thousand ſtreams in one,
One in a thousand on they fare,
   Now flaſhing to the sun,
     Now ſtill as beaſt in lair.

Now round the rock, now mounting o'er,
In lawless dance they win their way,
   Still seeming more and more
     To swell as we survey.

They win their way, and find their reſt
Together in their ocean home.
   From Eaſt and weary Weſt,
     From North and South they come.

They rufh and roar, they whirl and leap,
   Not wilder drives the wintry ftorm :
      Yet a ftrong law they keep,
         Strange powers their course inform.

Even so the mighty fky-born ftream :—
   Its living waters from above
      All marr'd and broken seem,
         No union and no love.

Yet in dim caves they haply blend,
   In dreams of mortals unespied :
      One is their awful End,
         One their unfailing Guide.

We that with eye too daring seek
   To scan their course, all giddy turn :—
      Not so the floweret meek,
         Harebell or nodding fern :

They from the rocky wall's fteep fide
   Lean without fear, and drink the spray ;
      The torrent's foaming pride
         But keeps them green and gay.

And Chrift hath lowly hearts, that reft
   Amid fallen Salem's rufh and ftrife ;
      The pure, peace-loving breaft
         Even here can find her life.

What though in harſh and angry note
   The broken flood chafe high? they muse
  On miſts that lightly float,
   On heaven-descending dews,

On virgin snows, the feeders pure
   Of the bright river's mountain springs :—
  And ſtill their prayers endure,
   And Hope sweet answer brings.

If of the Living Cloud they be
   Baptismal drops, and onward press
  Toward the Living Sea
   By deeds of holiness,

Then to the Living Waters ſtill
   (O joy with trembling!) they pertain,
  Joined by some hidden rill,
   Low in Earth's darkeſt vein.

Scorn not one drop: of drops the ſhower
   Is made, of ſhowers the waterfall:
  Of children's souls the Power
   Doomed to be Queen o'er all.

CHURCH DECORATIONS.

" I WILL not offer burnt-offerings without cost."

"WHY deck the high cathedral roof
　　With foliage rich and rare,
With crowns and flowerets far aloof,
　　To none but angels fair?

"Why for the lofty Altar hide
　　Thy gems and gold in ſtore?
Why spread the burniſhed pall so wide
　　Upon the chancel floor?"

Nay, rather aſk, why duteous boy
　　And mother-loving maid
Scarce in their filial gifts find joy,
　　If nought of theirs be paid:

Why hearts, that true love-tokens need
　　For brother or for friend,
Count not the coſt with careful heed,
　　But haſte their all to spend:

Aſk why of old the favored king
　　Inquired the Temple's price,
Not bearing to his Lord to bring
　　An unbought sacrifice.

Yea, lowly fall, and of thy Lord
  In filence afk and dread,
Why praised He Mary's ointment, poured
  Upon his Sacred Head.

ELIJAH AT SAREPTA.

"Make me thereof a little cake first, and bring it unto me, and after make for thee and for thy son."

Lo, caft at random on the wild sea sand
    A child low wailing lies:
Around, with eye forlorn and feeble hand,
    Scarce heeding its faint cries,
The widowed mother in the wilderness
Gathers dry boughs, their laft sad meal to bless.

But who is this that comes with mantle rude
    And vigil-wafted air?
Who to the famifhed cries, "Come give me food,
    I with thy child would fhare?"
She bounteous gives: but hard he seems of heart,
Who of such scanty ftore would crave a part.

Haply the child his little hand holds forth,
    That all his own may be.—

Nay, simple one, thy mother's faith is worth
    Healing and life to thee.
That handful given, for years insures thee bread;
That drop of oil shall raise thee from the dead.

For in yon haggard form He begs unseen,
    To whom for life we kneel:
One little cake He asks with lowly mien,
    Who blesses every meal.
Lavish for Him, ye poor, your children's store
So shall your cruise for many a day run o'er.

THE EMPTY CHURCH.

"THE blind and the lame came to him in the temple."

WHY should we grudge the hour and house of prayer
    To Christ's own blind and lame,
  Who come to meet Him there?
Better, be sure, his altar-flame
Should glow in one dim wavering spark,
Than quite die down, and leave his temple drear and dark.

"But in our Psalm their choral answers fail."
    Nay, but the heart may speak,
    And to the holy tale
Respond aright in silence meek.

And well we know, bright angel throngs
Are by, to swell those whisperings into warbled songs.

What if the world our two or three despise?
　　They in his name are here,
　　To whom in suppliant guise
Of old the blind and lame drew near.
Beſide his royal courts they wait
And aſk his healing hand; we dare not close the gate.

MISCELLANEOUS.

MISCELLANEOUS.

VIGILS.

IT is the fall of eve;
  And the long tapers now we light
And watch: for we believe
Our LORD may come at night.
    Adeſte Fideles.

  An hour—and it is Seven,
And faſt away the evening rolls:
  O, it is dark in heaven,
But light within our souls.
    Veni Creator Spiritus!

  Hark! the old bell ſtrikes Eight!
And ſtill we watch with heart and ear,
  For as the hour grows late,
The Day-ſtar may be near.
    Jubilate Deo!

  Hark! it is knelling Nine!
But faithful eyes grow never dim;

And ſtill our tapers ſhine,
And ſtill ascends our hymn.
    Cum Angelis!

The watchman crieth Ten!
My soul, be watching for the Light,
    For when he comes again,
'Tis as the thief at night.
    Nisi Dominus!

By the old bell—Eleven!
Now trim thy lamps, and ready ſtand;
    The world to ſleep is given,
But JESUS is at hand.
    De Profundis!

At midnight—is a cry!
Is it the bridegroom draweth near?
    Come quickly, LORD, for I
Have long'd thy voice to hear!
    Kyrie Eleison!

Could ye not watch One hour?
Be ready: or the bridal train
    And bridegroom, with his dower,
May sweep along in vain.
    Miserere mei!

By the old ſteeple—Two!
And now I know the day is near!

Watch—for his word is true,
And JESUS may appear!
   Dies Irae!

Three—by the drowsy chime!
And joy is nearer than at firſt.
   O, let us watch the time
When the firſt light ſhall burſt!
   Sursum Corda.

Four—and a ſtreak of day!
At the cock-crowing He may come;
   And ſtill to all I say,
Watch—and with awe be dumb.
   Fili David!

Five!—and the tapers now
In rosy morning dimly burn!
   Stand, and be girded thou,
Thy LORD will yet return!
   Veni JESU!

Hark! tis the Matin call!
Oh, when our LORD ſhall come again
   At prime or even-fall,
Bleſt are the wakeful men!
   Nunc dimittis.

A. C. Coxe.

NOTE.—The Latin lines, at the end of every stanza, are the titles of chaunts appropriate to the several hours. *Adeste:* Hither ye faithful.—*Veni Creator:* Come Holy Ghost.—*Jubilate Deo:* The 100th Psalm.—*Cum Angelis:* Therefore with angels and archangels, &c.—*Nisi Dominus:* Unless the Lord keep the city, the Watchman waketh but in vain.—*De Profundis:* Out of the depths, Ps. 130.—*Kyrie Eleison:* Lord have mercy upon us.—The *Miserere:* Ps. 57.—*Dies Irae:* The day of wrath.—*Sursum Corda:* Lift up your hearts.—*Fili David:* Son of David, have mercy upon us.—*Veni Jesu:* Come Lord Jesus—come quickly.—*Nunc Dimittis:* Now Lord lettest thou thy servant depart in peace, Luke 2. 29.

PENITENCE.

DEEPEN the wounds thy hands have made
   In this weak, helpless soul,
Till mercy, with its balmy aid,
   Descend to make me whole.

I see the exceeding broad command,
   Which all contains in one :
Enlarge my heart to underſtand
   The myſtery unknown.

O that, with all thy saints, I might
   By sweet experience prove
What is the length, and breadth, and height,
   And depth of perfect love !
                            C. Wesley.

GOING TO CHRIST.

"Him that cometh unto me, I will in no wise cast out."—
John 6: 37.

JUST as I am! without one plea
But that thy blood was fhed for me,
And that thou bid'ft me come to Thee,—
Oh Lamb of God, I come!

Juft as I am,—and waiting not
To rid my soul of one dark blot,
To Thee, whose blood can cleanse each spot—
Oh Lamb of God, I come!

Juft as I am—though toffed about
With many a conflict, many a doubt—
Fightings within, and fears without—
Oh Lamb of God, I come!

Juft as I am—poor, wretched, blind,
Sight, riches, healing of the mind,
Yea, all I need, in Thee to find,—
Oh Lamb of God, I come!

Juft as I am—Thou wilt receive,
Wilt welcome, pardon, cleanse, relieve,
Because thy promise I believe—
Oh Lamb of God, I come!

Juft as I am—thy love unknown
Has broken every barrier down;
Now to be thine, yea, thine alone,
Oh Lamb of God, I come!

Charlotte Elliot.

LOVE OF GOD.

THOU Grace divine, encircling all
  A soundless, fhoreless sea!
Wherein at laft, our souls fhall fall,
  O Love of God moft free!

When over dizzy fteeps we go,
  One soft hand blinds our eyes,
The other leads us safe and flow,
  O Love of God moft wise!

And though we turn us from thy face,
  And wander wide and long,
Thou hold'ft us ftill in thine embrace,
  O Love of God moft ftrong!

The saddened heart, the reftless soul
  The toilworn frame and mind,
Alike confess thy sweet control,
  O Love of God moft kind!

But not alone thy care we claim,
  Our wayward steps to win :
We know thee by a dearer name,
  O Love of God within !

And filled and quickened by thy breath,
  Our souls are ſtrong and free
To rise o'er ſin, and fear, and death,
  O Love of God, to thee !

EVENING PRAYER.

I COME to Thee to-night,
  In my lone closet where no eye can see
And dare to crave an interview with Thee,
  Father of love and light.

Softly the moonbeams ſhine
On the ſtill branches of the ſhadowy trees,
While all sweet sounds of evening on the breeze
  Steal through the ſlumbering vine.

Thou gav'ſt the calm repose
That rests on all ; the air, the birds, the flower,
The human spirit in its weary hour
  Now at the bright day's close.

'Tis Nature's time for prayer;
The silent praises of the glorious sky,
And the earth's orisons profound and high
　　To Heaven their breathings bear.

With them my soul would bend
In humble reverence at thy Holy Throne,
Trusting the merits of thy Son alone
　　Thy sceptre to extend.

If I this day have striven
With thy blest spirit, or have bowed the knee
To aught of earth in weak idolatry
　　I pray to be forgiven.

If in my heart has been
An unforgiving thought, or word, or look
Though deep the malice which I scarce could brook
　　Wash me from the dark sin.

If I have turned away
From grief or suffering which I might relieve,
Careless the cup of water e'en to give
　　Forgive me Lord I pray.

And teach me how to feel
My sinful wanderings with a deeper smart;
And more of mercy and of grace impart
　　My sinfulness to heal.

Father! my soul would be
Pure as the drops of eve's unsullied dew—
And as the ſtars whose nightly course is true—
　　So would I be to Thee.

Not for myself alone
Would I these bleſſings of thy love implore;
But for each penitent the wide earth o'er
　　Whom Thou haſt called thine own.

And for my heart's beſt friends,
Whose ſteadfaſt kindness o'er my painful years
Has watched to soothe affliction's griefs and tears,
　　My warmeſt prayer ascends.

Should o'er their path decline
The light of gladness, or of hope, or health,
Be Thou their solace, and their joy, and wealth,
　　As they have long been mine.

And now, O Father, take
The heart I caſt with humble faith on Thee,
And cleanse its depths from each impurity,
　　For my Redeemer's sake.

Anonymous.

EVENING HYMN.

THE night is come; like to the day,
Depart not thou, great God, away.
Let not my fins black as the night,
Eclipse the luftre of thy light.
Keep ftill in my horizon: for to me
The sun makes not the day, but Thee.
Thou whose nature cannot fleep,
On my temples sentry keep:
Guard me 'gainft those watchful foes,
Whose eyes are open while mine close.
Let no dreams my head infeft
But such as Jacob's temples bleft.
Whilft I do reft, my soul advance;
Make my fleep a holy trance:
That I may, my reft being wrought,
Awake into some holy thought.
And with as active vigor run
My course, as doth the nimble sun.
Sleep is a death, O make me try,
By fleeping, what it is to die:
And as gently lay my head
On my grave as now my bed.
Howe'er I reft, great God, let me
Awake again at laft with Thee.

And thus assur'd, behold I lie
Securely, or to wake or die.
These are my drowsy days; in vain
I do now wake to sleep again:
O come that hour, when I shall never
Sleep thus again, but wake for ever.
Sir Thomas Browne.

PRAYER.

ERE the morning's busy ray
   Call you to your work away;
Ere the silent evening close
Your wearied eyes in sweet repose;
To lift your heart and voice in prayer
Be your FIRST and LATEST care.

He, to whom the prayer is due,
From heaven his throne shall smile on you;
Angels sent by Him shall tend,
Your daily labor to befriend,
And their nightly vigils keep
To guard you in the hour of sleep.
Bishop Mant.

OH Lord! how happy should we be,
If we could leave our cares to Thee,
If we from self could reſt :
And feel at heart that One above,
In perfect wisdom, perfect love
Is working, for the beſt.

For when we kneel and caſt our care
Upon our God in humble prayer,
With ſtrengthened souls we rise.
Sure that our Father who is nigh
To hear the ravens when they cry
Will hear his children's cries.

Oh! would these reſtless hearts of ours
The leſſon learn from birds and flowers
And learn from self to cease;
Leave all things to our Father's will,
And in his mercy truſting ſtill
Find in each trial, peace.

Anonymous.

MY TIMES ARE IN THY HAND.

FATHER, I know that all my life
  Is portioned out for me,
And the changes that will surely come,
  I do not fear to see;
But I afk Thee for a present mind
  Intent on pleafing Thee.

I afk Thee for a thoughtful love,
  Through conftant watching wise,
To meet the glad with joyful smiles,
  And to wipe the weeping eyes;
And a heart at leisure from itself,
  To sooth and sympathize.

I would not have the reftless will
  That hurries to and fro,
Seeking for some great thing to do,
  Or secret thing to know;
I would be treated as a child,
  And guided where I go.

Wherever in the world I am,
  In whatsoe'er eftate,
I have a fellowfhip with hearts
  To keep and cultivate;

And a work of lowly love to do,
  For the Lord on whom I wait.

So I aſk Thee for the daily ſtrength,
  To none that aſk denied.
And a mind to blend with outward life,
  While keeping at thy ſide,
Content to fill a little space,
  If Thou be glorified.

And if some things I do not aſk
  In my cup of bleſſing be,
I would have my spirit fill'd the more
  With grateful love to Thee—
And careful, less to serve Thee much,
  Than to please Thee PERFECTLY.

There are briars besetting every path,
  Which call for patient care;
There is a cross in every lot,
  And an earneſt need for prayer;
But a lowly heart that leans on Thee
  Is happy anywhere.

In a service which thy love appoints,
  There are no bonds for me;
For my secret heart is taught "the truth"
  That makes thy children "free;"
And a life of self-renouncing love,
  Is a life of liberty.

Anna Letitia Waring.

IN having all things and not Thee, what have I?
  Not having Thee, what have my labors got?
Let me enjoy but Thee, what further crave I?
  And having Thee alone what have I not?
I wish not sea nor land; nor would I be
Possessed of heaven, heaven unpossessed of Thee.

Great God! Thou art the flowing spring of light;
  Enrich mine eyes with thy refulgent ray;
Thou art my path; direct my steps aright,
  I have no other light, no other way;
I'll trust my God, and Him alone pursue:
His law shall be my path, his heavenly light my clue.
Quarles.

EXCELLENCY OF CHRIST.

HE is a path, if any be misled;
  He is a robe, if any naked be;
If any chance to hunger, He is bread;
  If any be a bondman, He is free;
  If any be but weak, how strong is He!
To dead men life He is, to sick men health;
To blind men sight, and to the needy wealth;
A pleasure without loss, a treasure without stealth.
Giles Fletcher.

HARK! my soul, how every thing
Strives to serve our beauteous King;
Each a double tribute pays,
Sings its part, and then obeys.

Nature's chief and sweeteſt choir,
Him with cheerful notes admire;
Chanting every day their lauds,
While the grove their song applauds.

Though their voices lower be,
Streams have too their melody;
Night and day they warbling run,
Never pause, but ſtill ſing on.

All the flowers that gild the spring,
Hither their ſtill muſic bring;
If heaven bless them, thankful, they
Smell more sweet, and look more gay.

Only we can scarce afford,
This ſhort office to our Lord;
We, on whom his bounty flows,
All things gives, and nothing owes.

Wake, for ſhame, my ſlothful heart,
Wake, and gladly ſing thy part:

Learn of birds and springs and flowers,
How to use thy noble powers.

Call all nature to thy aid,
Since 'twas He all nature made;
Join in one eternal song
Who to one God all belong.

CALM, PEACE, AND LIGHT.

THERE is a Calm the Poor in Spirit know,
That softens sorrow, and that sweetens woe;
There is a Peace that dwells within the breaſt,
When all without is ſtormy and diſtreſt;
There is a Light that gilds the darkeſt hour,
When dangers thicken and when tempeſts lower,
That calm, to faith and hope and love is given,
That peace remains when all beſide is riven,
That light ſhines down to man direct from Heaven.

SONNET.

"O speak good of the Lord, all ye works of his, in all places of his dominions."—*Psalm* 103 : 22.

ANSWER, with all thy pulses, throb and speak,
Thou tender, palpitating heart of God!
Through earth, through air, and caves of ocean broad,
All thronged with myriad beings, ſtrong or weak
In terror, or deep love! Fluſh on the cheek
Of morn, breathe sweet from evening's dewy sod!
Tremble in muſic, 'mid the choral ode
That from the soft vale to the mountain peak
Whispers or thunders!—Art Thou cold, or dead,
Or vengeful?—Huſh! a holy ſilence reigns:
That our own heart, ſtilling our throbbing veins,
And only with its own aſſurance fed,
May be itself thy answer and abode,
O tender, palpitating heart of God!

Chauncy Hare Townſhend.

SONNET.

"ALL things work together for good to them that love God."—
Romans 8: 28.

OH, what a load of struggle and distress
 Falls off before the Cross ! The feverish care ;
The wish that we were other than we are ;
The sick regrets ; the yearnings numberless ;
The thought, "this might have been," so apt to press
On the reluctant soul ; even past despair,
Past sin itself,—all—all is turned to fair
Ay, to a scheme of ordered happiness,
So soon as we love God, or rather know
That God loves us ! . . . Accepting the great pledge
Of his concern for all our wants and woe,
We cease to tremble upon danger's edge ;
While varying troubles form and burst anew,
Safe in a Father's arms we smile as infants do !
Chauncy Hare Townshend.

SONNET.

"WHAT is truth?"—*St. John* 18: 38.

OH, how we pine for truth! for something more
Than hufks of learning! How did ancient Greece
Hang on the virtuous lips of Socrates,
Turning from words more sounding to adore
The wisdom that sent souls to their own ftore
For knowledge. So let us our hearts release!
'Tis time the jargon of the schools fhould cease—
Errors that rot Theology's deep core,
Lying at the base of things. Down, down muft fall
The glittering edifice, cemented much
With blood, yet baseless. At Truth's fimple touch
All the vain fabric will be fhattered —— all!
But not the Bible! Nature there is ftored,
And God! Eternal is the Saviour's Word!

Chauncy Hare Townfhend.

PRAYER.

LORD, what a change within us one short hour
   Spent in thy presence will avail to make!
What heavy burdens from our bosoms take!
What parchéd grounds refresh, as with a shower!
We kneel, and all around us seems to lower;
   We rise, and all, the distant and the near,
   Stands forth in sunny outline, brave and clear;
We kneel, how weak! we rise, how full of power!
Why, therefore, should we do ourselves this wrong,
Or others—that we are not always strong—
That we are ever overborne with care—
   That we should ever weak or heartless be,
Anxious or troubled—when with us is prayer,
   And joy, and strength, and courage are with *Thee?*
                                              Trench.

ACCESS TO GOD EVERY WHERE.

THEY who seek the throne of grace,
Find that throne in every place ;
If we live a life of prayer,
God is present every where.

In our ſickness or our health,
In our want or in our wealth,
If we look to God in prayer,
God is present every where.

When our earthly comforts fail,
When the foes of life prevail,
'Tis the time for earneſt prayer ;—
God is present every where.

Then, my soul, in every ſtrait
To thy Father come and wait ;
He will answer every prayer
God is present every where.

Anon.

PERFECT IN LOVE.

"WHOSO feareth is not made perfect in love. Perfect love casteth out fear."—1 *John* 4: 18.

"PERFECT in love!"—Lord, can it be,
  Amidst this state of doubt and sin?
While foes so thick without, I see,
  With weakness, pain, disease within:
    Can perfect love inhabit here,
    And strong in faith, extinguish fear?

O, Lord! amidst this mental night,
  Amidst the clouds of dark dismay,
Arise! arise! shed forth thy light,
  And kindle love's meridian day.
    My Saviour God to me appear,
    So love shall triumph over fear.

THE CHILDREN'S DESIRE.

I THINK when I read the sweet ftory of old,
How when Jesus was here among men,
He once called little children as lambs to his fold—
I fhould like to have been with them then.
I wifh that his hands had been placed on my head
That his arms had been thrown around me;
And that I might have seen his kind look, when He said,
" Let the little ones come unto me."

Yet ftill to his footftool in faith I may go,
And there afk for a fhare of his love;
And I know if I earneftly seek Him below,
I fhall see Him and hear Him above—
In that beautiful place, He is gone to prepare,
For all those who are wafhed and forgiven;
And many dear children are gathering there,
" For of such is the kingdom of heaven."

Anonymous.

LIFE.

IT is not life upon thy gifts to live,
But, to grow fixed with deeper roots in Thee;
And when the sun and shower their bounties give,
To send out thick-leaved limbs; a fruitful tree,
Whose green head meets the eye for many a mile,
Whose moss-grown arms their rigid branches rear,
And full-faced fruits their blushing welcome smile
As to its goodly shade our feet draw near;
Who tastes its gifts shall never hunger more,
For tis the Father spreads the pure repast,
Who, while we eat, renews the ready store,
Which at his bounteous board must ever last;
For none the bridegroom's supper shall attend,
Who will not hear and make his word their friend.

Jones Very.

P

FOR DIVINE STRENGTH.

FATHER, in thy myſterious presence kneeling,
  Fain would our souls feel all thy kindling love,
For we are weak, and need some deep revealing
  Of Truſt, and Strength, and Calmness, from above.

Lord, we have wandered forth through doubt and sorrow,
  And Thou haſt made each ſtep an onward one;
And we will ever truſt each unknown morrow,—
  Thou wilt suſtain us till its work is done.

In the heart's depths, a peace serene and holy
  Abides, and when pain seems to have her will,
Or we despair,—O may that peace rise ſlowly,
  Stronger than agony, and we be ſtill.

Now, Father, now, in thy dear presence kneeling,
  Our spirits yearn to feel thy kindling love:
Now make us ſtrong, we need thy deep revealing
  Of Truſt, and Strength, and Calmness, from above.
                                            S. *Johnson.*

THE CONFLICT OF LIFE.

ONWARD, Chriſtian, though the region
　　Where thou art be drear and lone :
God hath set a guardian legion
　　Very near thee,—press thou on !

Liſten, Chriſtian, their Hosanna
　　Rolleth o'er thee,—" God is Love."
Write upon thy red-cross banner,
　　" Upward ever,—heaven's above."

By the thorn-road, and none other,
　　Is the mount of viſion won ;
Tread it without ſhrinking, brother !
　　Jesus trod it,—press thou on !

By thy truſtful, calm endeavor,
　　Guiding, cheering, like the sun,
Earth-bound hearts thou ſhalt deliver :
　　O, for their sake, press thou on !

Be this world the wiser, ſtronger,
　　For thy life of pain and peace ;
While it needs thee, O no longer
　　Pray thou for thy quick release ;

Pray thou, Christian, daily, rather,
  That thou be a faithful son;
By the prayer of Jesus,—" Father,
  Not my will, but thine, be done!"
S. Johnson.

SPIRITUAL NEEDS.

I WANT the spirit of power within,
  Of love, and of a healthful mind:
Of power to conquer every sin,
  Of love to God and all mankind;
Of health that pain and death defies,
Most vigorous when the body dies.

O, that the Comforter would come,
  Nor visit as a transient guest,
But fix in me his constant home,
  And keep possession of my breast;
And make my soul his loved abode,
The temple of indwelling God!
C. Wesley.

JESUS, the only thought of thee
    With sweetness fills my breaft,
But sweeter far it is to see,
    And on thy beauty feaft.
No sound, no harmony so gay,
    Can art of mufic frame,
No thought can reach, no words can say
    The sweets of thy bleft name.

Jesus, our hope when we repent,
    Sweet source of all our grace;
Sole comfort in our banifhment
    O what when face to face!
Jesus! that name inspires my mind
    With springs of life and light;
More than I afk in thee I find,
    And languifh in delight.

No art nor eloquence of man
    Can tell the joys of love;
Spirits alone can underftand
    What they in Jesus prove.
Thee then I'll seek, retired apart,
    From world and bufiness free
When these fhall knock, I'll fhut my heart,
    And keep it all for thee.

Before the morning light I'll come,
With Magdalen, to find,
In sighs and tears, my Jesus' tomb,
And there refresh my mind.
My tears upon his grave shall flow,
My sighs the garden fill,
Then at his feet myself I'll throw,
And there I'll seek his will.

O THOU whose wise paternal Love
Hath cast my active vigor down,
Thy choice I thankfully approve,
And prostrate at thy gracious throne
I offer up my life's remains,
I choose the state my God ordains.

Cast as a broken vessel by,
Thy will I can no longer do,
But while a daily death I die,
Thy power I can in weakness show
My patience shall thy glory raise
My stedfast woe proclaim thy praise.

Steele.

ADORATION.

I LOVE my God, but with no love of mine,
    For I have none to give;
I love thee, Lord; but all the love is thine,
    For by thy life I live.
I am as nothing, and rejoice to be
Emptied, and loft, and swallowed up in thee.

Thou, Lord, alone, art all thy children need,
    And there is none befide;
From Thee the ftreams of bleffedness proceed,
    In Thee the bleft abide,—
Fountain of life, and all-abounding grace,
Our source, our centre, and our dwelling-place.
                      Madame Guyon.

FRIEND SORROW.

DO not cheat thy heart, and tell her
    "Grief will pass away—
"Hope for fairer times in future,
    "And forget to-day."

Tell her, if you will, that Sorrow
    Need not come in vain—
Tell her, that the leſſon taught her
    Far outweighs the pain.

Cheat her not with the old comfort
    "Soon ſhe will forget."
Bitter truth, alas! but matter
    Rather for regret.
Bid her not seek other pleasures,
    Turn to other things.
But rather nurse her cagéd Sorrow
    Till the captive ſings.

Rather bid her go forth bravely,
    And the ſtranger greet;
Not as foe, with ſhield and buckler,
    But as dear friends meet.
Bid her with a ſtrong clasp hold her
    By her duſky wings:
And ſhe'll whisper low and gently,
    Bleſſings that ſhe brings.
                  A. A. Procter.

LABOR AND REST.

"Two hands upon the breaſt, and labor is paſt."—*Russian Proverb.*

"TWO hands upon the breaſt,
    And labor's done:
Two pale feet croſſed in reſt—
    The race is won:
Two eyes with coin-weights ſhut,
    And all tears cease:
Two lips where grief is mute
    And wrath at peace."
So pray we oftentimes, mourning our lot;
God in his kindness answereth not.

"Two hands to work addreſt
    Aye for his praise:
Two feet that never reſt
    Walking his ways:
Two eyes that look above
    Still, through all tears:
Two lips that breathe but love,
    Nevermore fears."
So cry we afterwards, low at our knees:
Pardon those erring prayers! Father, hear these!

D. M. Muloch.

GOD IS LOVE.

EARTH, with her ten thousand flowers,
Air, with all its beams and fhowers,
All around, and all above,
Hath this record, "God is love."

Sounds among the vales and hills,
In the woods, and by the rills,
All these songs, beneath, above,
Have one burthen, "God is love."

All the charities that ftart
From the fountains of the heart,
These are voices from above,
Sweetly whispering, "God is love."

Earth with her ten thousand flowers,
Air, with all its beams and fhowers,
All are voices from above,
Loudly sounding, "God is love."

COULD'ST THOU NOT WATCH ONE HOUR?

THY night is dark—behold the ſhade was deeper
  In the old garden of Gethsemane,
When that calm voice awoke the weary ſleeper,
  —Could'ſt thou not watch one hour alone with me?

O, thou so weary of thy self-denials,
  And so impatient of thy little cross,
Is it so hard to bear thy daily trials,
  To count all earthly things a gainful loss?

What if thou *always* suffer tribulation,
  And if thy Chriſtian warfare *never* cease;
The gaining of the quiet habitation,
  Shall gather thee to everlaſting peace.

But here we all muſt suffer, walking lonely
  The path that Jesus once himself hath gone;
Watch thou in patience through this hour only,
  This one dark hour before the eternal dawn.

The captive's oar may pause upon the galley,
  The soldier ſleep beneath his plumed creſt,
And peace may fold her wing o'er hill and valley,
  But thou, O Chriſtian, muſt not take thy reſt.

Thou muſt walk on, however man upbraid thee,
   With Him who trod the wine-press all alone;
Thou wilt not find one human hand to aid thee,
   One human soul, to comprehend thine own.

Heed not the images forever thronging
   From out the foregone life thou liveſt no more,
Faint-hearted mariner, ſtill art thou longing
   For the dim line of the receding ſhore.

Wilt thou find reſt of soul in thy returning
   To that old path thou haſt so vainly trod?
Haſt thou forgotten all thy weary yearning
   To walk among the children of thy God?

Faithful and ſteadfaſt in their consecration,
   Living by that high faith to thee so dim,
Declaring before God their dedication,
   So far from thee, because so near to him.

Can'ſt thou forget thy Chriſtian superscription—
   " Behold we count them happy which endure?"
What treasure would'ſt thou in the land Egyptian,
   Repass the ſtormy water to secure?

And wilt thou yield thy sure and glorious promise
   For the poor fleeting joys earth can afford?
No hand can take away the treasure from us
   That reſts within the keeping of the Lord.

Poor wandering soul—I know that thou art seeking
  Some eafier way, as all have sought before
To filence the reproachful inward speaking—
  Some landward path unto an ifland fhore!

The cross is heavy in thy human measure,
  The way too narrow for thine inward pride,
Thou can'ft not lay thine intellectual treasure
  At the low footftool of the Crucified.

O, that thy faithless soul, one hour only
  Would comprehend the Chriftian's perfect life,
Despised with Jesus, sorrowful and lonely,
  Yet calmly looking upward in its ftrife.

For poverty and self-renunciation,
  Their Father yieldeth back a thousand fold;
In the calm ftillness of regeneration,
  Cometh a joy they never knew of old.

In meek obedience to the heavenly Teacher,
  Thy weary soul can only find its peace,
Seeking no aid from any human creature;
  Looking to God alone for his release.

And He will come in his own time and power,
  To set his earneft-hearted children free;
Watch only through this dark and painful hour
  And the bright morning yet will break for thee.

THE SACRIFICE.

O ALL ye who pass by, whose eyes and mind
   To worldly things are sharp, but to me blind,—
To me, who took eyes that I might you find;—
    Was ever grief like mine?

Mine own apostle, who the bag did bear,
Though he had all I had, did not forbear
To sell *me* also, and to put me there.
    Was ever grief like mine?

Judas, dost thou betray me with a kiss?
Can'st thou find hell about my lips, and miss
Of life, just at the gates of life and bliss?
    Was ever grief like mine?

See, they lay hold on me; not with the hands
Of faith, but fury. Yet, at their commands,
I suffer binding, who have loosed *their* bands.
    Was ever grief like mine?

All my disciples flee; fear put a bar
Betwixt my friends and me. They leave that Star
That brought wise men out of the East from far.
    Was ever grief like mine?

Ah! how they scourge me! yet my tenderness
Doubles each lash. And yet, their bitterness
Winds up my grief to a mysteriousness.
    Was ever grief like mine?

Then on my head a crown of thorns I wear;
For these are all the grapes Zion doth bear,
Though I my vine planted and watered there.
    Was ever grief like mine?

So sits the earth's great curse, in Adam's fall,
Upon *my* head; so I remove it all
From th' earth unto my brows, and bear the thrall.
    Was ever grief like mine?

The soldiers also spit upon that face
Which angels did desire to have the grace,
And prophets, once, to see, but found no place.
    Was ever grief like mine?

But, O my God! my God! why leavest thou me,
Thy Son, in whom thou dost delight to be?
My God! My God!———
    Never was grief like mine!

Shame tears my soul, my body many a wound;—
Sharp nails pierce this, but sharper that confound;
Reproaches, which are free while I am bound.
    Was ever grief like mine?

Now heal thyself, Physician! now come down!
Alas! I did so, when I left my crown,
And Father's smile, for you to feel his frown.
    Was ever grief like mine?

Betwixt two thieves I spend my utmoſt breath,
As he that for some robbery suffereth.
Alas! what have I ſtolen from you? Death.
    Was ever grief like mine?

They gave me vinegar mingled with gall,—
But more with malice. Yet, when they did call,
With manna, angels' food, I fed them all.
    Was ever grief like mine?

Nay, after death, their spite ſhall further go;
For they will pierce my side, I full well know;—
That, as ſin came, so sacraments might flow.
    Was ever grief like mine?

But now I die. Now all is finiſhed—
My woe, man's weal: and now I bow my head.
Only let others say, when I am dead,
    Never was grief like mine!
      George Herbert.

THE CHARMER.

"WE need some Charmer, for our hearts are sore
    With longings for the things that may not be—
Faint for the friends that shall return no more
    Dark with distrust, or wrung with agony.

"What is this life? And what to us is Death?
    Whence came we? whither go? And where are those
Who in a moment stricken from our side
    Passed to that land of shadow and repose.

"Are they all dust? and dust must we become?
    Or are they living in some unknown clime?
Shall we regain them in that far-off home,
    And live anew beyond the waves of time?

"Oh man divine!—on thee our souls have hung,
    Thou wert our teacher in these questions high;
But ah! this day divides thee from our side,
    And veils in dust thy kindly guiding eye."

So spake the youth of Athens, weeping round
    When Socrates lay calmly down to die—
So spake the Sage, prophetic of the hour
    When Earth's fair Morning Star should rise on high.

They found him not, those youths of soul divine
  Long seeking, wandering, watching on life's shore:
Reasoning, aspiring, yearning for the light,
  Death came and found them—doubting as before.

But years passed on—and lo! the Charmer came
  Pure, silent, sweet as comes the silver dew—
And the world knew him not—he walked alone
  Encircled only by his trusting few.

Like the Athenian Sage—rejected, scorned,
  Betrayed, condemned, his day of doom drew nigh,
He drew his faithful few more closely round,
  And told them that *His* hour was come to die.

"Let not your heart be troubled," then He said:
  My Father's house has mansions large and fair;
I go before you to prepare your place;
  I will return to take you with me there.—

And since that hour the awful foe is charmed,
  And life and death are glorified and fair:
Whither He went we know—the way we know,
  And with firm step press on to meet Him there.

H. B. Stowe.

THE CALM OF THE SOUL.

WHEN winds are raging o'er the upper ocean,
    And billows wild contend with angry roar,
'Tis said, far down beneath the wild commotion,
    That peaceful stillness reigneth, evermore.

Far, far beneath, the noise of tempests dieth,
    And silver waves chime ever peacefully,
And no rude storm, how fierce soe'er it flieth,
    Disturbs the Sabbath of that deeper sea.

So to the heart that knows thy love, O Purest!
    There is a temple, sacred evermore,
And all the babble of life's angry voices,
    Dies in hushed stillness, at its peaceful door.

Far, far away, the roar of passion dieth,
    And loving thoughts rise calm and peacefully,
And no rude storm, how fierce soe'er it flieth,
    Disturbs the soul that dwells, O Lord, in thee.

O rest of rests! O peace, serene, eternal!
    Thou ever livest, and thou changest never;
And in the secret of thy presence dwelleth
    Fulness of joy, forever and forever.
H. B. Stowe.

WHEN I AWAKE I AM STILL WITH THEE.

STILL, still with Thee—when purple morning breaketh,
   When the bird waketh, and the shadows flee;
Fairer than morning, lovelier than the daylight,
   Dawns the sweet consciousness, *I am with Thee.*

Alone with Thee—amid the myftic shadows,
   The solemn hush of nature newly born;
Alone with Thee in breathless adoration,
   In the calm dew and freshness of the morn.

As in the dawning o'er the waveless ocean,
   The image of the morning ftar doth reft,
So in this ftillness, Thou beholdeft only
   Thine image in the waters of my breaft.

Still, ftill with Thee! as to each new-born morning
   A frefh and solemn splendor ftill is given,
So doth this bleffed consciousness awaking,
   Breathe, each day, nearness unto Thee and Heaven.

When finks the soul, subdued by toil, to flumber,
   Its clofing eye looks up to Thee in prayer;
Sweet the repose beneath thy wings o'erfhading
   But sweeter ftill, to wake and find Thee there.

So shall it be at last, in that bright morning,
  When the soul waketh, and life's shadows flee;
Oh! in that hour, fairer than daylight dawning,
  Shall rise the glorious thought, *I am with Thee!*

H. B. Stowe.

ORDINATION HYMN.

CHRIST to the young man said : " Yet one thing more ;
  If thou would'st perfect be,
Sell all thou hast and give it to the poor,
  And come and follow me! "

Within this temple Christ again, unseen,
  Those sacred words hath said,
And his invisible hands to-day have been
  Laid on a young man's head.

And evermore beside him on his way
  The unseen Christ shall move,
That he may lean upon his arm and say,
  " Dost thou, dear Lord, approve? "

Beside him at the marriage feast shall be,
  To make the scene more fair;
Beside him in the dark Gethsemane
  Of pain and midnight prayer.

O holy truft! O endless sense of reft!
Like the beloved John
To lay his head upon the Saviour's breaft,
And thus to journey on!

Longfellow.

HYMN FOR LENT.

O WEEP for them who never knew
    The mother of our love,
And fhed thy tears for orphan ones,
    Whom angels mourn above;
The wandering fheep—the ftraying lambs,
    When wolves were on the wold,
That left our Shepherd's little flock,
    And ventured from his fold.

Nay, blame them not! for them, the Lord
    Hath loved as well as you:
But O, like Jesus, pray for them
    Who know not what they do:
O plead as once the Saviour did,
    That we may all be one,
That so the cruel world may know
    The Father sent the Son.

O let thy Lenten litanies
  Be full of prayer for them!
O go ye to the scattered sheep
  Of Israel's parent stem!
O keep thy fast for Christendom!
  For CHRIST's dear body mourn;
And weave again the seamless robe,
  That faithless friends have torn.

Ye love your dear home-festivals,
  With every month entwined;
O weep for them whose sullen hearths
  No Christmas garlands bind!
Those Iceland regions of the faith
  No changing seasons cheer,
While our sweet paths drop fruitfulness,
  Through all the joyous year.

What though some borealis-beams
  On even them may flare;
Pray God the sunlight of his love
  May rise serenely there!
For flashy gleams, O plead the Lord
  To give his daily ray!
With heavenly light at morn and eve
  To thaw their wintry way.

O weep for those, on whom the Lord
  While here below did weep,

Left grievous wolves should enter in,
  Not sparing of his sheep;
And eat thy bitter herbs awhile,
  That when our Feast is spread,
These too—that gather up the crumbs,
  May eat the children's bread.
                              A. C. Coxe.

THE BLESSING AFTER SERVICE.

THE peace which God bestows,
  Through him who died and rose,
The peace the Father giveth through the Son,
  Be known in every mind,
  The broken heart to bind,
And bless each traveller as he journeys on.

  Ye who have known to weep,
  Where your beloved sleep,
Ye who have raised the deep, the bitter cry,
  God's blessing be as balm,
  The fevered soul to calm,
And wondrous peace the troubled mind supply.

  Young man, whose cheek is bright
  With nature's warmest light,

While youth and health thy veins with rapture swell
  Let the remembrance be
  Of thy God bleſt to thee,
Peace paſſing underſtanding guard thee well.

  Parents, whose thoughts afar,
  Turn where your children are,
In their ſtill graves, or beneath foreign ſkies,—
  This hour, God's bleſſing come
  Cheer the deserted home,
And peace, with dove-like wings, around you rise.

  Ere this week's ſtrife begin,
  The war without, within,
The God of Love, with spirit and with power,
  Now on each bended head,
  His wondrous bleſſing ſhed,
And keep you all through every troubled hour.

STRENGTH.

(To an Invalid.)

"WHEN I am weak, I'm ſtrong,"
    The great Apoſtle cried.
The ſtrength that did not to the earth belong,
    The might of Heaven supplied.

"When I am weak, I'm ſtrong,"
    Blind Milton caught that ſtrain,
And flung its victory o'er the ills that throng
    Round Age, and Want, and Pain.

"When I am weak, I'm ſtrong,"
    Each Chriſtian heart repeats;
These words will tune its feebleſt breath to song,
    And fire its languid beats.

O Holy Strength! whose ground
    Is in the heavenly land;
And whose supporting help alone is found
    In God's immortal hand!

O bleſſed! that appears
   When fleſhly aids are spent;
And girds the mind, when moſt it faints and fears,
   With truſt and sweet content.

It bids us caſt aſide
   All thoughts of leſſer powers;—
Give up all hopes from changing time and tide,
   And all vain will of ours.

We have but to confess
   That there's but one retreat:
And meekly lay each need and each diſtress
   Down at the Sovereign feet;—

Then, then, it fills the place
   Of all we hoped to do;
And sunken Nature triumphs in the Grace,
   That bears us up and through.

A better glow than health
   Fluſhes the cheek and brow,
The heart is stout with store of nameless wealth:—
   We can do all things now.

No less sufficience seek;
   All counsel less is wrong;
The whole world's force is poor, and mean, and weak;—
   "When I am weak, I'm strong."

                    N. L. Frothingham.

CALL TO THE PRODIGAL.

RETURN, O wandérer, return,
And seek thy Father's face;
Those new defires that in thee burn,
Were kindled by his grace.

Return, O wandérer, return,
Thy Saviour bids thee live;
Go to his bleeding feet and learn
How Jesus can forgive.

Return, O wandérer, return,
And wipe away the tear;
'Tis God who says, "No longer mourn,"—
Mercy invites thee near.
Collyer.

THE MYSTERY OF CHASTISEMENT.

"We glory also in tribulations."—*Romans* 5 : 3.

WITHIN this leaf, to every eye
    So little worth, doth hidden lie
Moſt rare and subtile fragrancy:

Would'ſt thou its secret ſtrength unbind?
Cruſh it, and thou ſhalt perfume find,
Sweet as Arabia's spicy wind.

In this dull ſtone, so poor, and bare
Of ſhape or luſtre, patient care
Will find for thee a jewel rare.

But firſt muſt ſkilful hands eſſay,
With file and flint, to clear away
The film, which hides its fire from day.

This leaf? this ſtone? It is thy heart:
It muſt be cruſhed by pain and smart,
It muſt be cleansed by sorrow's art—

Ere it will yield a fragrance sweet,
Ere it will shine, a jewel meet
To lay before thy dear Lord's feet.
                                            S. Wilberforce.

PROVIDENCE.

SINCE all the coming scenes of time
   God's watchful eye surveys,
O who so wise to choose our lot,
   And regulate our ways?

Since none can doubt his equal love,
   Immeasurably kind,
To his unerring gracious will,
   Be every wish resigned.

Good when He gives, supremely good,
   Nor less when He denies;
E'en crosses from his sovereign hand,
   Are blessings in disguise.
                                            Hervey.

"MY TIMES ARE IN THY HAND."

Psalm 31: 15.

"My times are in thy hand,"
  My God, I'd have them there;
My life, my friends, my soul, I leave
  Entirely to thy care.

"My times are in thy hand,"
  Whatever they may be;
Pleasing or painful, dark or bright,
  As best may seem to Thee.

"My times are in thy hand,"
  Why should I doubt or fear?
My Father's hand will never cause
  His child a needless tear.

"My times are in thy hand,"
  I'll always trust in Thee:
And after death, at thy right hand
  I shall for ever be.

HE LEADS HIS OWN.

"I WILL lead them in the paths they have not known."
Isaiah 42 : 16.

HOW few who, from their youthful day,
Look on to what their life may be;
Painting the vifions of the way
In colors soft, and bright, and free.
How few who to such paths have brought
The hopes and dreams of early thought!
For God, through ways they have not known,
Will lead his own.

The eager hearts, the souls of fire,
Who pant to toil for God and man;
And view with eyes of keen defire
The upland way of toil and pain;
Almoſt with scorn they think of reſt,
Of holy calm, of tranquil breaſt,
But God, through ways they have not known,
Will lead his own.

A lowlier taſk on them is laid,—
With love to make the labor light;

And there their beauty they muft fhed
  On quiet homes and loft to fight.
Changed are their vifions high and fair,
Yet calm, and ftill, they labor there ;
  For God, through ways they have not known,
    Will lead his own.

The gentle heart that thinks with pain,
  It scarce can lowlieft tafks fulfil ;
And, if it dared its life to scan,
  Would afk but pathway low and ftill.
Often such lowly heart is brought
To act with power beyond its thought ;
  For God, through ways they have not known,
    Will lead his own.

And they, the bright, who long to prove,
  In joyous path, in cloudless lot,
How frefh from earth their grateful love
  Can spring without a ftain or spot,—
Often such youthful heart is given
The path of grief, to walk in Heaven ;
  For God, through ways they have not known,
    Will lead his own.

What matter what the path fhall be ?
  The end is clear and bright to view ;
We know that we a ftrength fhall see,
  Whate'er the day may bring to do,
  R

We see the end, the house of God,
But not the path to that abode;
For God, through ways they have not known,
Will lead his own.

CORRECTION NEEDED.

"WHEREFORE doth a living man complain, a man for the punishment of his fins?"—*Lamentations* 3: 39.

WISH not, dear friends, my pain away;
Wifh me a wise and thankful heart,
With God, in all my griefs, to ftay,
Nor from his loved correction ftart.

The deareft offering He can crave,
His portion in our souls to prove,
What is it to the gift He gave,
The only Son of his dear love?

In life's long fickness, evermore
Our thoughts are tofling to and fro:
We change our pofture o'er and o'er,
But cannot reft, nor cheat our woe.

Were it not better to lie ftill,
Let Him ftrike home, and bless the rod?
Never so safe as when our will
Yields, undiscerned by all, to God.
                                    Keble.

DETAINED FROM THE SANCTUARY.

"For I had gone with the multitude; I went with them to the house of God, with the voice of joy and praise, with a multitude that kept holy day."—*Psalm* 42 : 4.

SWEET Sabbath bells! I love your voice,—
  You call me to the house of prayer;
Oft have you made my heart rejoice,
  When I have gone to worfhip there.

But now, a prisoner of the Lord,
  His hand forbids, I cannot go;
Yet may I here his love record,
  And here the sweets of worfhip know.

Each place alike is holy ground,
  Where prayer from humble souls is poured;
Where praise awakes its filver sound,
  Or God is filently adored.

His sanctuary is the heart,—
There, with the contrite, will he reſt ;
Lord, come, a Sabbath frame impart,
And make thy temple in my breaſt.

CLINGING TO JESUS.

"SEEING then we have a great high priest that is passed into the heavens, Jesus, the Son of God, let us hold fast our profession."
Heb. 4: 14.

HOLY Saviour, friend unseen,
Since on thy arm thou bid'ſt me lean,
Help me throughout life's varying scene,
   By faith to cling to thee!

Bleſt with this fellowſhip divine,
Take what thou wilt, I'll ne'er repine ;
E'en as the branches to the vine,
   My soul would cling to thee!

Far from her home, fatigued, oppreſt,
Here ſhe has found her place of reſt ;
An exile ſtill, yet not unbleſt,
   While ſhe can cling to thee !

Oft, when I seem to tread alone
Some barren waſte with thorns o'ergrown,
Thy voice of love, in tendereſt tone,
        Whispers, " ſtill cling to me!"

Though faith and hope may oft be tried,
I aſk not, need not, aught beſide ;
How safe, how calm, how satisfied,
        The soul that clings to thee!

Bleſt is my lot, whate'er befall ;
What can diſturb me, what appall,
Whilſt as my rock, my ſtrength, my all,
        Saviour! I cling to thee?

COMMITTING THE SOUL TO THE SAVIOUR.

" INTO thy hand I commit my spirit ; thou hast redeemed me, O Lord God of truth."—*Psalm* 31 : 5.

MY spirit on thy care,
  Bleſt Saviour, I recline ;
Thou wilt not leave me to despair,
  For thou art love divine.

In thee I place my truſt,
  On thee I calmly reſt;
I know thee good,—I know thee juſt,
  And count thy choice the best.

Whate'er events betide,
  Thy will they all perform;
Safe in thy breaſt my head I hide
  Nor fear the coming ſtorm.

Let good or ill befall,
  It muſt be good for me;
Secure of having thee in all,
  Of having all in thee.

LORD, I BELIEVE.

"Lord, I believe; help thou mine unbelief."—*Mark* 9: 24.

YES, I do feel, my God, that I am thine;
  Thou art my joy—myself, mine only grief;
Hear my complaint, low bending at thy ſhrine,—
"Lord, I believe; help thou mine unbelief."

Unworthy, even, to approach so near,
  My soul lies trembling like a summer's leaf;
Yet, O forgive! I doubt not, though I fear,—
  "Lord, I believe; help thou mine unbelief."

True, I am weak, ah, very weak; but then
  I know the source whence I can draw relief;
And, though repulsed, I still can plead again,—
  "Lord, I believe; help thou mine unbelief."

O, draw me nearer; for, too far away,—
  The beamings of thy brightness are too brief;
While faith, though fainting, still have strength to pray,—
  "Lord, I believe; help thou mine unbelief."
                                        Monsell.

DOWN the dark future, through long generations,
  The sounds of war grow fainter, and then cease;
And like a bell with solemn, sweet vibrations,
  I hear once more the voice of Christ say, "Peace!"

Peace! and no longer, from its brazen portals
  The blast of war's great organ shakes the skies;
But beautiful as songs of the immortals,
  The holy melodies of love arise.
                                        Longfellow.

CHRIST UNCHANGING.

"Jesus Christ, the same yesterday, and to-day, and forever."
Heb. 13 : 8.

CHANGE is written everywhere,
 Time and death o'er all are ranging;
Seasons, creatures, all declare,
 Man is mortal, earth is changing.

Life, and all its treasures, seem
 Like a sea in conſtant motion;
Thanks for an eternal beam
 Shining o'er the pathless ocean.

One by one, although each name
 Providence or death will sever;
Jesus Chriſt is ſtill the same,
 Yeſterday, to-day, forever.

"I SHALL BE SATISFIED."

NOT here!—not here! Not where the sparkling waters
    Fade into mocking sands as we draw near:
Where in the wilderness each footstep falters—
    "I shall be satisfied;" but, O! not here!

Not here—where all the dreams of bliss deceive us,
    Where the worn spirit never gains its goal;
Where, haunted ever by the thought that grieves us,
    Across us floods of bitter memory roll.

There is a land where every pulse is thrilling
    With rapture earth's sojourners may not know,
Where heaven's repose the weary heart is stilling,
    And peacefully life's time-tossed currents flow.

Far out of sight, while yet the flesh infolds us,
    Lies the fair country where our hearts abide,
And of its bliss is nought more wondrous told us
    Than these few words—"I shall be satisfied."

Satisfied! Satisfied! The spirit's yearning
    For sweet companionship with kindred minds—
The silent love that here meets no returning—
    The inspiration which no language finds—

Shall they be satisfied? The soul's vague longing—
The aching void which nothing earthly fills?
O! what defires upon my soul are thronging
As I look upward to the heavenly hills:

Thither my weak and weary fteps are tending—
Saviour and Lord! with thy frail child abide!
Guide me toward Home, where all my wanderings ending,
I shall see thee, and "*fhall be satisfied.*"

———◆———

FROM "THE CHERUBIC PILGRIM,"

The Dew and the Rose.

"GOD'S spirit falls on me as dew-drops on a rose,
If I but like a rose to him my heart unclose.

The Tabernacle.

The soul wherein God dwells—what church can holier
be?—
Becomes a walking tent of heavenly majefty.

The Difference.

Ye know God but as Lord, hence *Lord* his name with ye,
I feel him but as Love, and LOVE his name with me.

Chriſt must be Born in Thee.
Though Chriſt a thousand times in Bethlehem be born,
If He's not born in thee, thy soul is ſtill forlorn.

The Outward Profiteth Not.
The cross on Golgotha will never save thy soul,
The cross in thine heart alone can make thee whole.

The only Want's in Thee.
Ah, would thy heart but be a manger for the birth,
God would once more become a child upon the earth.

The Seasons of the Day.
In Heaven is the day, in Hell below, the night;
'Tis twilight here on Earth: conſider this aright!

The loveliest Tone.
In all Eternity, no tone can be so sweet
As where man's heart with God in unison doth beat.

Magnet and Steel.
God is a magnet ſtrong; my heart, it is the ſteel,
'Twill always turn to Him, if once his touch it feel.

Love's Transubstantiation.
Whate'er thou loveſt, man, that too become thou muſt:
God—if thou loveſt God; Duſt—if thou loveſt duſt.

The Well is Deep.
Why fhould'ft thou cry for drink? The fountain is in thee,
Which so thou ftopp'ft it not, will flow eternally.
John 4: 11.

To Theologians.
Within this span of time, God's name ye will unfold,
Which in eternities can never quite be told.

Bleffedness.
The soul that's truly bleft, knows not of selfifhness;
She is one light with God, with God one Bleffedness.

Old and Young.
Thou smileft at the child that cryeth for his toys,
Are they less toys, old man, that cause thy griefs and joys?

It is Here.
Why travel over seas to find what is so near?
Love is the only good; love and be bleffed here.

Spiritual Sun and Moon.
Be Jesus thou my Sun, and let me be thy moon,
Then will my darkeft night be changed to brighteft noon.

The Spiritual Mount.
I am a mount in God, and muft myself ascend,
Shall God, to speak to me, upon my top descend.

Life in Death.
In God alone is Life, without God is but death,
An endless godless life were but a life in death.

Wisdom a Child.
We afk how Wisdom can thus play in children's guise?
Why Wisdom *is* a child, so's every man that's wise.

The Valley and the Rain.
Let but thy heart, O man! become a valley low,
And God will rain on it till it will overflow.

Divine Music.
A quiet patient heart that meekly serves his Lord,
God's finger joys to touch; it is his harpfichord.

How we can see God.
God dwelleth in a light far out of human ken,
Become thyself that light, and thou wilt see Him then.

God's Work and Reft.
God never yet has worked, nor did He ever reft,
His reft is aye his work, his work is aye his reft.

Great Gifts and small Receivers.
Our great God always would the greateft gifts impart,
If but his greateft gifts found not so small a heart.

To the Reader.

Let, Reader, this suffice. But fhould'ft thou wifh for more,
Then read in *thine own heart* a page of myftic lore.
Angelus Silesius.

FROM ALGER'S ORIENTAL POETRY.

The Beatific Vifion.

THE dazzling beauty of the Loved One fhines unseen,
And self's the curtain o'er the road; away, O screen!

The Luminous Truth.

"Who will give me his heart," said God, " my love he fhall find."
With that speech a resplendent sun fell into my mind.

The Two Travellers.

Says God: " Who comes towards Me an inch through doubtings dim,
In blazing light I do approach a yard towards him."

All is Safe.

Whatever road I take, it joins the ftreet
Which leadeth all who walk it Thee to meet.

The Divine Judgment.
God asks, not " To what sect did he belong ? "
But " Did he do the right, or love the wrong ? "

Precept without Practice.
Who learns and learns, but acts not what he knows,
Is one who ploughs and ploughs, but never sows.

A Rank in Joys.
My heart! abstain thou from the senses' dear wine-bowl;
Diviner joys thy God intends shall through thee roll.

Nip the Bud.
A sprout of evil, ere it has struck root,
With thumb and finger one up-pulls:
To start it, when grown up and full of fruit,
Requires a mighty yoke of bulls.

Swift Opportunity.
A thousand years a poor man watched
Before the gate of Paradise:
But while one little nap he snatched,
It oped and shut. Ah! was he wise?

Squandered Youth.
Ah, five-and-twenty years ago had I but planted seeds of trees,
How now I should enjoy their shade, and see their fruit swing in the breeze!

The Pilgrim to Deity.

Heedless, allured, one moment I forgot my goal:
A thousand years it ſtretched the journey of my soul.

The Pledge and the Thing.

This life is a dim pledge of friendſhip from our God:
Give me the Friend, and the pledge may ſink in the sod.

Cling not to aught that may be snatched from o'er the rim;
One fairy tale was all that Jemschid took with him.

God All in All.

Exempt from luſt, exempt from love of pelf,
The wise man acts unconscious of himself.
He cares not for his actions' consequence,
But feeds devotion's fire with pure incense.

God is his gift, his sacrifice is God;
God is his sacrificial knife and rod,
Himself, his altar, altar's flame, the sword;
God also is the worſhip's sole reward.

THE BEGGAR'S COURAGE.

TO heaven approached a Súfi saint,
   From groping in the darkness late,
And, tapping timidly and faint,
   Besought admiſſion at God's gate.

Said God, " Who seeks to enter here ? "
   " 'Tis I, dear Friend," the saint replied,
And trembled much with hope and fear.
   " If it be *thou*, without abide."

Sadly to earth the poor saint turned,
   To bear the scourgings of life's rods ;
But aye his heart within him yearned
   To mix and lose its love in God's.

He roamed alone through weary years,
   By cruel men ſtill scorned and mocked,
Until, from faith's pure fires and tears,
   Again he rose, and modeſt knocked.

Aſked God, " Who now is at the door ? "
   " It is thyself, beloved Lord ! "
Answered the saint, in doubt no more,
   But clasped and rapt in his reward.

THE SAYINGS OF RABIA.

I.

A pious friend one day of Rabia afked
How fhe had learned the truth of Allah wholly:
By what inftructions was her memory tafked?
How was her heart eftranged from the world's folly?

She answered, "Thou, who knoweft God in parts,
Thy spirit's moods and proceffes can tell:
I only know that, in my heart of hearts,
I have despised myself, and loved Him well."

II.

Some evil upon Rabia fell;
And one, who loved and knew her well,
Murmured, that God, with pain undue,
Should ftrike a child so fond and true.
But fhe replied, "Believe and truft
That all I suffer. is moft juft.
I had, in contemplation, ftriven
To realize the joys of heaven;
I had extended Fancy's flights
Through all that region of delights;
Had counted, till the numbers failed,
The pleasures on the bleft entailed;
Had sounded the ecftatic reft

I should enjoy on Allah's breast;
And for those thoughts I now atone,
They were of something of my own,
And were not thoughts of Him alone."

III.

When Rabia unto Mecca came,
She stood awhile apart, alone;
Nor joined the crowd, with hearts of flame,
Collected round the sacred stone.

She like the rest, with toil had crossed
The waves of water, rock, and sand;
And now, as one long tempest-tossed,
Beheld the Raala's promised land.

Yet in her eyes no transport glistened:
She seemed with shame and sorrow bowed:
The shouts of prayer she hardly listened;
She beat her heart, and cried aloud,—

"O heart! weak follower of the weak,
That thou should'st traverse land and sea,
In this far place that God to seek
Who long ago had come to thee!"

IV.

Round holy Rabia's suffering bed
　The wise men gathered, gazing gravely.
" Daughter of God! " the youngeſt said,
　" Endure the Father's chaſtening bravely:
They who have ſteeped their souls in prayer,
Can every anguiſh calmly bear."

She answered not, and turned aſide,
　Though not reproachfully or sadly.
" Daughter of God!" the eldeſt cried,
　" Suſtain thy Father's chaſtening gladly:
They who have learned to pray aright,
From Pain's dark well draw up delight."

Then spake ſhe out, " Your words are fair;
　But oh! the truth lies deeper still:
I know not, when absorbed in prayer,
　Pleasure or pain, or good or ill:
They who God's face can underſtand,
Feel not the workings of his hand."
　　　　　　　　　　　　" *Heart Songs.*"

THE TWISTER.

"A TWISTER in twifting would twift him a twift,
And, twifting his twift, seven twifts he doth twift;
If one twift, in twifting, untwift from the twift,
The twift untwifting, untwifts the twift."

A RAVELLED rainbow overhead
  Lets down to life its varying thread:
Love's blue, — joy's gold, — and, fair between,
Hope's fhifting light of emerald green;
With, either fide, in deep relief,
A crimson Pain, — a violet Grief.
Would'ft thou, amid their gleaming hues,
Clutch after those, and these refuse?
Believe, — as thy beseeching eyes
Follow their lines, and sound the fkies, —
There, where the fadelefs glories fhine,
An unseen angel twifts the twine.

And be thou sure, what tint soe'er
The broken rays beneath may wear,
It needs them all, that, broad and white,
God's love may weave the perfect light!

Mrs. A. D. T. Whitney.

THE HEAVENLY SOWING.

SOWER Divine!
Sow the good seed in me,
Seed for eternity.
'Tis a rough barren soil,
Yet by Thy care and toil,
Make it a fruitful field
An hundred fold to yield.
Sower Divine,
Plough up this heart of mine!

Sower Divine!
Quit not this wretched field
Till Thou haft made it yield;
Sow Thou by day and night,
In darknefs and in light.
Stay not Thy hand, but sow;
Then fhall the harveft grow.
Sower Divine,
Sow deep this heart of mine!

Sower Divine!
Let not this barren clay,
Lead Thee to turn away;

Let not my fruitleſsneſs
Provoke Thee not to bleſs;
Let not this field be dry,
Refreſh it from on high.
Sower Divine,
Water this heart of mine!

     Rev. Dr. H. Bonar.

ON THE DEATH OF HIS SON.

Lyra Germanica.

THO'RT mine, yes, ſtill thou art mine own!
 Who tells me thou art loſt?
But yet thou art not mine alone,
 I own that He who croſſ'd
My hopes, hath greateſt right in thee;
Yea, though He aſk and take from me
Thee, O my son, my heart's delight,
My wiſh, my thought, by day and night.

Ah might I wiſh, ah might I choose,
 Then thou, my ſtar, ſhould'ſt live,
And gladly for thy sake I'd lose
 All else that life can give.
Oh fain I'd say: Abide with me,
The sunſhine of my house to be,
No other joy but this I crave,—
To love thee, darling, to my grave!

Thus saith my heart, and means it well,
    God meaneth better ſtill;
My love is more than words can tell,
    His love is greater ſtill;
I am a father, He the Head
And Crown of fathers, whence is ſhed
The life and love from which have sprung
All bleſſed ties in old and young.

I long for thee, my son, my own!
    And He who once hath given,
Will have thee now beſide His throne,
    To live with Him in Heaven.
I cry, alas! my light, my child!
But God hath welcome on him smiled,
And said, "*My* child, I keep thee near,
For there is nought but gladneſs here."

Oh bleſſed word, oh deep decree,
    More holy than we think!
With God no grief or woe can be,
    No bitter cup to drink,
No ſickening hopes, no want or care,
No hurt can ever reach him there;
Yes, in that Father's ſheltered home
I know that sorrow cannot come.

We paſs our nights in wakeful thought
    For our dear children's sake;
All day our anxious toil hath sought
    How beſt for them to make

A future safe from care or need,
Yet seldom do our schemes succeed;
How seldom does their future prove
What we had planned for those we love!

How many a child of promise fair
   Ere now hath gone aſtray,
By ill example taught to dare
   Forsake Chriſt's holy way.
Oh fearful the reward is then,
The wrath of God, the scorn of men!
The bittereſt tears that e'er are ſhed
Are his who mourns a child miſled.

But now I need not fear for thee,
   Where thou art, all is well;
For thou thy Father's face doth see,
   With Jesus thou doſt dwell!
Yes, cloudleſs joys around him ſhine,
His heart ſhall never ache like mine;
He sees the radiant armies glow
That keep and guide us here below.

He hears their ſinging evermore
   His little voice too ſings,
He drinks of wisdom's deepeſt lore,
   He speaks of secret things,
That we can never see or know,
Howe'er we seek or ſtrive below,
While yet amid the miſts we ſtand
That veil this dark and tearful land.

Oh that I could but watch afar,
  And hearken but awhile
To that sweet song that hath no jar,
  And see his heavenly smile,
As he doth praise the holy God,
Who made him pure for that abode!
In tears of joy full well I know
This burdened heart would overflow.

And I fhould say: Stay here, my son,
  My wild laments are o'er,
O well for thee that thou haft won,
  I call thee back no more;
But come, thou fiery chariot, come,
And bear me swiftly to that home,
Where he with many a loved one dwells,
And evermore of gladnefs tells!

Then be it as my Father wills,
  I will not weep for thee;
Thou liveft, joy thy spirit fills,
  Pure sunfhine thou doft see,
The sunfhine of eternal reft;
Abide, my child, where thou art bleft;
I with our friends will onward fare,
And, when God wills, fhall find thee there.

Paul Gerhardt. 1650.

QUIET FROM GOD.

"IF He giveth quiet, who can make trouble?" — *Job* 34 : 29.

QUIET from God! It cometh not to ftill
   The vaft and high aspirings of the soul,
The deep emotions which the spirit fill,
   And speed its purpose onward to the goal;
     It dims not youth's bright eye,
     Bends not joy's lofty brow,
     No guiltlefs ecftasy
     Need in its presence bow.

It comes not in a sullen form, to place
   Life's greateft good in an inglorious reft ;
Through a dull, beaten track its way to trace,
   And to lethargic flumber lull the breaft ;
     Action may be its sphere,
     Mountain paths — boundlefs fields,
     O'er billows its career:
     This is the power it yields.

To sojourn in the world, and yet apart;
   To dwell with God, yet ftill with man to feel ;
To bear about forever in the heart
   The gladnefs which His spirit doth reveal ;

Not to deem evil gone
From every earthly scene ;
To see the ſtorm come on,
But feel His ſhield between.

It giveth not a ſtrength to human kind,
To leave all suffering powerleſs at its feet,
But keeps within the temple of the mind
A golden altar, and a mercy seat ;
A spiritual ark,
Bearing the peace of God
Above the waters dark,
And o'er the desert's sod.

How beautiful within our souls to keep
This treasure, the All-Merciful hath given;
To feel, when we awake, and when we ſleep,
Its incense round us, like a breeze from heaven !
Quiet at hearth and home,
Where the heart's joys begin ;
Quiet where'er we roam,
Quiet around, within.

Who ſhall make trouble ? — not the evil minds
Which like a ſhadow o'er creation lower,
The spirit peace hath so attunéd, finds
There feelings that may own the Calmer's power ;
What may ſhe not confer,
E'en where ſhe muſt condemn ?
They take not peace from her,
She may speak peace to them !

SEEN AND UNSEEN.

THE wind ahead, the billows high,
A whited wave, but sable sky,
And many a league of tossing sea,
Between the hearts I love and me.

The wind ahead: day after day
These weary words the sailors say;
To weeks the days are lengthened now, —
Still mounts the surge to meet our prow.

Through longing day and lingering night
I still accuse Time's lagging flight,
Or gaze out o'er the envious sea,
That keeps the hearts I love from me.

Yet, ah, how shallow is all grief!
How instant is the deep relief!
And what a hypocrite am I,
To feign forlorn, to 'plain and sigh!

The wind ahead? The wind is free!
Forevermore it favoreth me, —
To shores of God still blowing fair,
O'er seas of God my bark doth bear.

This surging brine *I* do not sail,
This blaſt adverse is not my gale;
'Tis here I only seem to be,
But really sail another sea,—

Another sea, pure ſky its waves,
Whose beauty hides no heaving graves,—
A sea all haven, whereupon
No haplefs bark to wreck hath gone.

The winds that o'er my ocean run,
Reach through all heavens beyond the sun;
Through life and death, through fate, through time,
Grand breaths of God they sweep sublime.

Eternal trades, they cannot veer,
And blowing, teach us how to ſteer;
And well for him whose joy, whose care,
Is but to keep before them fair.

Oh, thou God's mariner, heart of mine,
Spread canvas to the airs divine!
Spread sail! and let thy Fortune be
Forgotten in thy Deſtiny!

For Deſtiny pursues us well,
By sea, by land, through heaven or hell;
It suffers Death alone to die,
Bids life all change and chance defy.

Would earth's dark ocean suck thee down?
Earth's ocean thou, O Life, shalt drown,
Shalt flood it with thy finer wave,
And, sepulchred, entomb thy grave!

Life loveth life and good : then trust
What most the spirit would, it must ;
Deep wishes, in the heart that be,
Are blossoms of necessity.

A thread of Law runs through thy prayer,
Stronger than iron cables are ;
And Love and Longing toward her goal,
Are pilots sweet to guide the soul.

So Life must live, and Soul must sail,
And Unseen over Seen prevail,
And all God's argosies come to shore,
Let ocean smile, or rage and roar.

And so, 'mid storm or calm, my bark
With snowy wake still nears her mark ;
Cheerly the trades of being blow,
And sweeping down the wind I go.

D. A. Wasson.

CHEERFULNESS.

BE merry, man, and tak not sair to mind
　　The wavering of this wretched world of sorrow;
To God be humble, to thy friend be kind,
　　And with thy neighbours gladly lend and borrow;
　　His chance to-night, it may be thine to-morrow.
Be blyth in hearte for my aventure,
　　For oft with wise men it has been said aforow,
Without Gladnefs availes no Treasure.

Make thee gude cheer of it that God thee sends;
　　For warld's gain without health naught avails;
Nae gude is thine save only that thou spends,
　　Remanant all thou bruikes but with bails;
　　Seek to solace when sadnefs thee affails;
In dolour long thy life may not endure,
　　Wherefore of comfort set up all thy sails;
Without Gladnefs availes no Treasure.

Follow on pity, flee trouble and debate,
　　With famous folkes hald thy company;
Be charitable and hum'le in thine eftate,
　　For warldly honour laftes but a day.
　　For trouble in earth tak no melancholy;

Be rich in patience, if thou in gudes be poor;
Who lives merrily he lives mightily;
Without Gladnefs availes no Treasure.
> *William Dunbar.* 1479-1520.

FORGIVENESS.

THE faireft action of our human life
    Is scorning to revenge an injury;
For who forgives without a further ftrife,
    His adversary's heart to him doth tie.
And 'tis a firmer conqueft truly said,
To win the heart than overthrow the head.

If we a worthy enemy do find,
    To yield to worth it muft be nobly done;
But if of baser metal be his mind,
    In base revenge there is no honour won.
Who would a worthy courage overthrow,
And who would wreftle with a worthlefs foe?

We say our hearts are great, and cannot yield;
    Because they cannot yield, it proves them poor:
Great hearts are tafk'd beyond their power, but seld
    The weakeft lion will the loudeft roar.
Truth's school for certain doth this same allow,—
High-heartednefs doth sometimes teach to bow.

A noble heart doth teach a virtuous scorn:
　To scorn to owe a duty overlong;
To scorn to be for benefits forborne;
　To scorn to lie, to scorn to do a wrong;
To scorn to bear an injury in mind;
To scorn a free-born heart, flave-like to bind.

But if for wrongs we needs revenge muft have,
　Then be our vengeance of the nobleft kind:
Do we his body from our fury save,
　And let our hate prevail againft his mind?
What can 'gainft him a greater vengeance be,
Than make his foe more worthy far than he?
　　　　　　　　Lady Elizabeth Carew. 1613.

PATIENCE.

PATIENCE! Why, 'tis the soul of peace:
Of all the virtues, 'tis neareſt kin of heaven:
It makes men look like gods. The beſt of men
That e'er wore earth about him was a sufferer,—
A soft, meek, patient, humble, tranquil spirit;
The firſt true gentleman that ever breathed.
       Thomas Dekkar. 1630.

GOD.

SHAKE hands with earth, and let your soul respect
Her joys no farther, than her joys reflect
Upon her Maker's glory; if thou swim
In wealth, see Him in all; see all in Him:
Sink'ſt thou in want, and is thy small cruise spent?
See Him in want, enjoy Him in content;
Conceiv'ſt Him lodg'd in crofs, or loft in pain?
In prayer and patience find Him out again.
       Francis Quarles.

HEAVEN.

THER is lyf withoute ony deth,
And ther is youthe without ony elde;
And ther is alle manner welthe to welde:
And ther is reft without ony travaille;
And ther is pees without ony ftrife,
And ther is alle manner lykinge of lyf: —
And ther is bright somer ever to se,
And ther is nevere wynter in that countrie: —
And ther is more worfhipe and honour,
Than evere hade kynge other emperour.
And ther is grete melodie of aungeles songe,
And ther is preyfing hem amonge.
And ther is alle manner frendfhipe that may be,
And ther is evere perfect love and charite;
And ther is wisdom without folye,
And ther is honefte without vileneye.
Al these a man may joyes of hevene call;
Ac yutte the moft sovereyn joye of alle
Is the fighte of Godde's bright face,
In wham refteth alle mannere grace.

Richard Rolle. About 1350.

LOVE.

O WEDDING-GUEST! this soul hath been
   Alone on a wide, wide sea;
So lonely 'twas, that God himself
   Scarce seeméd there to be.

O sweeter than the marriage-feaft,
   'Tis sweeter far to me,
To walk together to the kirk
   With a goodly company!

To walk together to the kirk,
   And all together pray,
While each to his great Father bends:
   Old men, and babes, and loving friends,
   And youths and maidens gay!

Farewell, farewell; but this I tell
   To thee, thou wedding-gueft;
He prayeth well who loveth well
   Both man and bird and beaft.

He prayeth beft who loveth beft
   All things both great and small;
For the dear God who loveth us,
   He made and loveth all.

Coleridge.

HEAR what God, the Lord, hath spoken:
  O my people, faint and few,
Comfortless, afflicted, broken,
  Fair abodes I build for you;
Scenes of heartfelt tribulation
  Shall no more perplex your ways;
You shall name your walls salvation,
  And your gates shall all be praise.

There, like streams that feed the garden
  Pleasures without end shall flow;
For the Lord, your faith rewarding,
  All his bounty shall bestow:
Still in undisturbed possession
  Peace and righteousness shall reign;
Never shall you feel oppression,
  Hear the voice of war again.

Ye, no more your suns descending
  Waning moons no more shall see;
But your griefs forever ending,
  Find eternal noon in me:
God shall rise, and shining o'er you,
  Change to day the gloom of night;
He, the Lord, shall be your glory,
  God your everlasting light.

Cowper.

INDEX TO FIRST LINES.

	PAGE
A pious friend one day of Rabia aſked	290
Ah! dearest Lord! I cannot pray	69
All ye who seek a certain cure	79
All ye who seek, in hope and love	99
Answer with all thy pulses, throb and speak	234
At the Cross her station keeping	129
Banished the House of sacred rest	191
Bright Angels who attend	30
Bright Cherubim and Seraphim	98
Bright were the mornings first impearl'd	97
Change is written every where	280
Cheer up desponding soul	28
Christ to the young man said : Yet one thing more	261
Come, Holy Ghost, and through each heart	8
Come my soul awake 'tis morning	172
Come, O Creator Spirit blest	20
Come wandering sheep, O come	73
Cometh sunshine after rain	158
Creator Spirit, by whose aid	52
Darker and darker fall around	127

312   *Index.*

	PAGE
Dear Angel! ever at my side	125
Dear Soul, couldst thou become a child	145
Deepen the wounds thy hands have made	220
Depart awhile each thought of care	19
Do not cheat thy heart, and tell her	247
Down the dark future, through long generations	279
Earth with her ten thousand flowers	250
Ere the morning's busy ray	227
Eternity, Eternity!	147
Exempt from lust, exempt from love of pelf	288
Faith of our Fathers! living still	29
Father, I know that all my life	229
Father, in thy mysterious presence kneeling	242
Father of lights! one glance of thine	115
Fear not, O little flock, the foe	143
Five loving souls, each one as mine	205
From highest Heaven, the Father's Son	119
God liveth ever	150
God's Spirit falls on me	282
God, Thou art my Rock of strength	165
God whom I as love have known	175
Grant us a body pure within	17
Great Framer of the earth and sky	6
Hark my soul how every thing	232
Have mercy Thou, most gracious God	36
He is a path if any be misled	231
Head of the Hosts in glory	95
Hear what God, the Lord, hath spoken	310
Hear'st thou my soul what serious things	47
Holy Saviour, friend unseen	276
Holy Spirit! Lord of Light	51

Index. 313

	PAGE
Holy and innocent were all his ways	114
How few who from their youthful day	272
I come to Thee to-night	223
I love my God but with no love of mine	247
I think when I read the sweet story of old	240
I want the spirit of power within	244
I will not let Thee go	157
I worship thee, sweet Will of God	45
In caves of the lone wilderness thy youth	100
In having all things and not Thee, what have I	231
It is not life upon thy gifts to live	241
It is the fall of eve	217
Jerusalem, thou City blest	120
Jesu, I my Cross have taken	32
Jesu, the very thought of Thee	75
Jesus, the only thought of Thee	245
Just as I am! without one plea	221
Leave God to order all thy ways	170
Let us arise and watch ere dawn of light	9
Lift up your hearts	43
Lift up your heads ye mighty gates	141
Light! Light! Infinite Light!	74
Light of the soul, O Saviour blest	84
Lo! cast at random on the wild sea sand	212
Lo! fainter now lie spread the shades of night	11
Lo! He comes with clouds descending	89
Lo! on the slope of yonder shore	106
Lo! upon the altar lies	116
Look westward, pensive little one	200
Lord, I have fasted, I have prayed	186
Lord, in this dust thy sovereign voice	182
Lord of all power! at whose command	55

	PAGE
Lord of eternal purity	22
Lord of eternal truth and might	8
Lord what a change within us one short hour	237
Lovely flowers of martyrs, hail	114
Most High and Holy Trinity	163
My child, the counsels high attend	195
My God, accept my heart this day	31
My God, I love Thee not because	37
My Saviour what Thou didst of old	155
My smile is bright, my glance is free	189
My Soul! what hast thou done for God	61
My spirit longeth for Thee	27
My spirit on thy care	277
My times are in thy hand	271
Nigher still, and still more nigh	85
No track is on the sunny sky	133
Not here, not here, not where the sparkling waters	281
Now at the Lamb's high royal feast	83
Now doth the sun ascend the sky	4
Now let us sit and weep	78
Now rests her soul in Jesus' arms	176
Now while the herald bird of day	14
Now with the rising golden dawn	16
O all ye who pass by, whose eyes and mind	254
O blessed Saint, of snow-white purity	105
O blest Creator of the light	3
O bounteous Framer of the globe	50
O Captain of the Martyr Host	104
O Christ! the beauty of the angel worlds	101
O come and mourn with me awhile	81
O Faith! thou workest miracles	34
O for the happy days gone by	66

Index. 315

	PAGE
O Friend of souls, how well is me	168
O Heart of fire! misjudged by wilful man	187
O Holy Ghost, Thou fire divine	161
O how I fear Thee, living God	26
O how the thought of God attracts	23
Oh how we pine for truth for something more	236
O it is hard to work for God	39
O Jesu! Thou the beauty art	77
O Jesus! King most wonderful	76
Oh Lord! how happy should we be	228
Oh that it were as it was wont to be	92
O Thou pure light of souls that love	87
O Thou the Father's Image blest	10
O Thou true life of all that live	9
O Thou whose wise paternal Love	246
Oh turn those blessed points, all bathed	91
Onward Christian, through the region	243
O watchman will the night of sin	139
O weep for them who never knew	262
Oh what a load of struggle and distress	235
Our limbs with tranquil sleep refresh'd	5
Perfect in love, Lord can it be	239
Preserve, my Jesus, oh preserve	117
Prune thou thy words, the thoughts control	185
Pure Light of light! eternal Day	13
Pure, meek, with soul serene	108
Return, O wanderer, return	268
Rise, glorious Conqueror, rise	93
Rock of Ages, rent for me	88
Round holy Rabia's suffering bed	292
She once was a lady of honor and wealth	111
Shed kindly light amid the encircling gloom	184

	PAGE
Since all the coming scenes of time	270
Sing we the peerless deeds of martyr'd Saints	102
Soil not thy plumage, gentle dove	12
Soldiers of Christ! arise	59
Some evil upon Rabia fell	290
Star of the wide and pathless sea	131
Still, still with Thee, when purple morning breaketh	260
Sweet Sabbath bells, I love your voice	275
Tear not away the veil, dear friend	202
The Church is one wide harvest field	204
The dazzling beauty of the loved one	286
The light of love is round his feet	56
The Lord's eternal gifts	103
The night is come, like to the day	226
The night is dark—behold the shade was deeper	251
The pall of night o'ershades the earth	21
The peace which God bestows	264
The silver chord in twain is snapp'd	44
The star that heralds in the morn	18
Thee in the hymns of morn we praise	22
There is a calm the Poor in Spirit know	233
There is not on the earth a soul so base	181
They who seek the throne of grace	238
Thou art of all created things	135
Thou Grace divine, encircling all	222
Thou loving Maker of mankind	54
Thy word, O Lord, like gentle dews	153
To Christ, the Prince of Peace	80
To heaven approached a Súfi saint	289
To the hall of that feast came the sinful and fair	60
Two hands upon the breast	249
Upon our fainting souls distil	17

Index. 317

	PAGE
We need some Charmer, for our hearts are sore	257
We watch'd, as she linger'd all the day	109
What time the Saviour spread his feast	196
When Heaven in mercy gives thy prayers return	199
When I am weak, I'm strong	266
When I look back upon my former race	184
When I sink down in gloom or fear	190
When Rabia into Mecca came	291
When thou dost talk with God	71
When winds are raging o'er the upper ocean	259
What is the Church, and what am I	207
While Thou, O my God, art my help and defender	49
Why deck the high cathedral roof	211
Why dost thou beat so quick, my heart	64
Why haltest thus deluded heart	166
Why is thy face so lit with smiles	122
Why should we grudge the hour and house of prayer	213
Wish not dear friends my pain away	274
Within this leaf to every eye	269
Ye mist and darkness, cloud and storm	15
Yes, I do feel, my God, that I am thine	278

Supplement to Index.

A ravelled rainbow overhead	293
Be merry, man, and tak not sair to mind	304
O wedding-guest! this soul hath been	309
Patience! Why, 'tis the soul of peace	307
Quiet from God! It cometh not to still	299
Shake hands with earth, and let your soul respect	307
Sower Divine!	294
The wind ahead, the billows high	301
The fairest action of our human life	305
Ther is lyf withoute ony deth	308
Tho'rt mine, yes, still thou art mine own!	295

www.ingramcontent.com/pod-product-compliance
Lightning Source LLC
Chambersburg PA
CBHW021206230426
43667CB00006B/585